The Editors would like to express their gratitude to Audrey Harrow for assisting with the editing of this book and to Andrew Duncan and Marie McDermott for all their help with the word-processing.

Gender Perceptions and the Law

Edited by
DR. CHRISTINE R. BARKER,
ELIZABETH A. KIRK and
MONICA SAH
Department of Law,
University of Dundee

Routledge
Taylor & Francis Group
LONDON AND NEW YORK

First published 1998 by Dartmouth and Ashgate Publishing

Reissued 2018 by Routledge
2 Park Square, Milton Park, Abingdon, Oxon, OX14 4RN
711 Third Avenue, New York, NY 10017, USA

Routledge is an imprint of the Taylor & Francis Group, an informa business

A Library of Congress record exists under LC control number: 97039116

ISBN 13: 978-1-138-31640-9 (hbk)
ISBN 13: 978-0-429-45567-4 (ebk)

Contents

Foreword

The main aim of this collection of papers (and the lecture series upon which it is based) is to bring contemporary issues of law and legal policy out into wider debate. The papers collected in this book were presented at the annual Scrymgeour Lecture Series at the Department of Law, University of Dundee during session 1995-1996. The purpose of the Scrymgeour Lecture Series is to raise a particular theme for discussion which challenges existing perceptions of law and its role in society, and to contribute to debate on that theme in an informed and informative manner. The 1995-1996 Series focused on the theme "Gender and the Law" and benefited from the contribution of leading sociologists and lawyers on different aspects of the topic.

The papers focus on two main issues - the influence of gender on legal relationships and of the law on gender relationships - and are further unified by two common arguments.

The first argument is that gender roles within society (both social and economic) affect the legal rights of individuals and impact on the procedures they may/must go through to enforce their rights, or gain redress for wrongs done to them. In addition, stereotypical gender roles and existing legal procedures impact on the likelihood of any given individual succeeding in enforcing his or her rights or gaining redress.

The second argument is that the law does not recognise the social and economic situations in which men and women are placed, the result being that it perpetuates inequalities in their positions. Where attempts are made to ensure equality between the sexes the result is often the exact opposite. In seeking to ensure equality the legal system and the law treat individuals as equals operating in a vacuum. The system fails to consider the individual and group experiences of those before them and ignores the argument that equal treatment does not necessarily mean the same treatment, but can mean different treatment to ensure equality of result.

These arguments are discussed in the context of three areas of the law: family law, criminal law and equal rights. The first two chapters focus on family law and deal primarily with the very controversial issue of parental child custody rights, focusing on disputes between parents.

In the first chapter, Professor Carol Smart argues that the *Children Act 1989* diminishes the ability of women to acquire custody of their children when there has been an acrimonious breakdown of the marriage. This conclusion is reached on the basis of ground-breaking empirical research in which approximately 60 parents were interviewed soon after divorce and again one year later. The Act gives a free rein to the bargaining process under which parents negotiate for custody where there is a dispute over the residence of or contact with the children. This free rein is, however, tempered by the fact that the Act does not allow for account be taken of the past contributions of the respective parents in child care, instead it prescribes the welfare of the child as the determining factor of the negotiations. In so doing the Act seems to have adversely affected the bargaining power of mothers.

Professor Alastair Bissett-Johnson also focuses on family law issues by following up the case of child custody for professional women and investigating the controversial area of rights of surviving spouses to their deceased partner's estate. Like Professor Smart, Professor Bissett-Johnson argues that the courts, in applying the welfare of the child test, may disadvantage successful working mothers in child custody disagreements. In the case of succession rights, a similar argument has been made: the law has not adequately and fairly responded to changing demographic and social trends and when applied to current life situations may result in widows (or widowers) being less protected than they ought to be against the claims of adult children to the estate.

The next two chapters examine the gender difference in the area of crime. Professor Gerda Siann, a sociologist, begins the discussion by presenting the main theories explaining violent behaviour in women as contrasted with the explanations for violent behaviour in men. Professor Siann then considers how these explanations of aggression and violence can bias the outcomes of legal cases. Most interestingly, she notes how perceptions of women as inherently non-violent and submissive result in female offenders being labelled as social deviants or psychologically ill. Dr Neil Hutton picks up these theories and applies them to a particular case - gender bias in criminal sentencing. Sentencing is most often based upon the notion of "just deserts" which, as Dr Hutton notes, is tied to the seriousness of the crime. He argues that in at least some circumstances the "just deserts" rule leads to bias in that the effects of equivalent sentences as applied to individuals, or certain groups of individuals may vary widely to the extent that one individual or group of individuals (for example women) is consistently treated more harshly by the law. That is, either that the sentence, as narrowly construed by law, combined with their particular circumstances, leads to a total sentence which is harsher than the sentence others receive for the same or similar offences, or that a particular group within society is consistently found to commit particular offences which receive harsher sentences than equivalent offences. Dr Hutton then uses this fact to argue for more lenient sentences for female offenders and suggests that these can be justified, for example, by the special social role of women as the primary care-givers for children.

The last three chapters in the collection look at various aspects of the equal rights debate. Muriel Robison examines equal rights in the area of employment law. She focuses on the contribution of European law in promoting sex equality in the work place. Robison looks specifically at how Article 119 of the Treaty of Rome and the Equal Pay Directive have been implemented in UK domestic law. These provide for equal treatment in employment (including pay situations) for men and women. She argues that UK employment law has been pushed towards promoting sex equality in the workplace by the enforcement of such obligations by the European Court of Justice, a mechanism which the Equal Opportunities Commission does not hesitate to use.

Equal rights arguments are examined in relation to pornography and gay rights by Professor Beverley Brown and Dr David Evans respectively. Professor Brown views the debate on pornography as one which counterpoises women's access to equal rights with free speech. She argues that one's view of the social context of pornography determines whether it should or should not be controlled. As a "speech act", pornography is justified by liberals under the right of free speech in a democratic society. If it is viewed merely as an act, however, then it is arguably an obstacle to equality. Although Dr Evans's contribution focuses on sexuality, rather than gender, he also examines the age of consent debate for gay males according to equal rights arguments. The paper focuses on homosexuality as a civil right of citizenship which can not, as such, be contravened.

The editors are grateful to all the contributors to the Scrymgeour Lecture Series for permitting their papers to be included in this collection.

[illegible] applied to individuals or [illegible] groups of individuals may [illegible] to the extent that [illegible] group of [illegible] individuals, for example [illegible] by the law. That is, [illegible] compared with their particular circumstances [illegible] which [illegible] that [illegible] offenders [illegible] particular [illegible]

The last three chapters in the collection [illegible] the aspect of [illegible] law. [illegible] of [illegible] and law in [illegible] equality in the workplace. [illegible] Robinson, looking specifically at [illegible] the Equal Pay Directive have been incorporated in UK domestic law. [illegible] for men and women. [illegible] employment [illegible] in the workplace by the [illegible] the Equal Opportunities [illegible]

[illegible] parliamentary [illegible] and [illegible] Hickey [illegible] equality with [illegible] the social [illegible] of [illegible] whether [illegible] should not be [illegible] under the [illegible] in [illegible] however [illegible] and [illegible] equality [illegible]

The [illegible] to the [illegible]

1 Negotiating Parenthood: Bargaining in the Shadow of a New Law

PROFESSOR CAROL SMART, School of Sociology and Social Policy, University of Leeds

My title for this paper is *Negotiating Parenthood: Bargaining in the shadow of a new law,* and the recent legislation to which I refer is the Children Act 1989 which was enacted in England and Wales in 1992. My interests are in the private law provisions of the Act and I first propose to discuss the background to the development of this legislation because this will provide the foundation for my later remarks based on an ongoing empirical research project.[1] The discussion in the second part of this paper will therefore be drawn from preliminary research findings based on interviews with divorced or separated parents, and in my conclusion I shall give some tentative consideration to issues of social (in)justice.

The background to the Children Act 1989

There were two main social developments that foregrounded the emergence of the private law provisions of the Children Act. These two elements were, first, a shift in understanding of what the welfare of the child actually means and how the welfare of children can best be met in cases of divorce and separation. Secondly, there has been a very important shift in the concept of social justice. In referring to social justice I want to focus quite specifically on the question of equal rights between men and women and the related issue of the rise of the men's movement in the UK.

1. The shift in the concept of the welfare of the child

In overviewing the shifts and changes in the concept of the welfare of the child since the early nineteenth century, one can identify four main headings under which changing ideas can be grouped. Broadly speaking one can see a shift from *Father Right* to *The Tender Years Doctrine* and then to *Maternal Preference.*[2] More recently we have entered a phase one can identify as the *Co-Parenting Preference*. As this history is fairly familiar I shall deal with it quite briefly.

The concept of the welfare of the child was a very small element of the law on husbands and wives in the nineteenth century. As divorce became more of a possibility for the upper classes, the issue of children did not constitute a major dilemma to policy makers because of the presumption that children were the property of fathers.[3] Indeed it was assumed that it was automatically in the welfare of the child to be with the father who was their legal guardian. This premise began gradually to be modified by the *Tender Years Doctrine*, which arose from the early campaign of Caroline Norton[4] in which she argued that a mother's love was vital to the welfare of children. In practice this meant that policy ultimately shifted towards accepting the idea that children under seven years of age would be better off staying with their mothers because only mothers could provide the necessary kind of love and affection. Once over the age of seven, it was thought that children were more adequately looked after by fathers.

This doctrine, which lasted from the turn of the century until (approximately) the Second World War, in turn gave way to what has become known as *Maternal Preference*. After the war and into the early 1970s, a pattern emerged where there was a simple presumption that the welfare of the child was best met by being placed with the mother, unless she could be shown to be a very inadequate mother.

Each of these shifts coincided with other important social and cultural changes. Most significant amongst these changes has been the altered status of women[5] and the changing nature of childhood.[6] Shifts in these areas have not been linear nor simple and they have interacted with each other to produce different outcomes at different moments. Thus there have been tensions between women's changing status in the labour market, their status as wives and their identity and role as mothers. At the same time childhood has been extended and the needs of the infant have become more precisely specified whilst the very concept of the adolescent has been created. Naturally these changes could not occur without changes to the status of husbands and fathers - but these changes seem to have lagged behind other changes,[7] and we may only just now be realising the extent to which these identities and roles have started to change and will need to change further in future.

Arguably it could be said that in the post-war decades men's relationships to families were very one-dimensional. They were expected to be breadwinners and even their role as fathers was overdetermined by the need to be economic providers. If a biological father left his family, it was assumed that the main problem was a financial one. Policy issues addressed the problem of financial support for divorced mothers and their children. The Finer Committee[8] was set up precisely to address this growing problem in combination with the problem of supporting unwed and widowed mothers. Moreover, legal policy at this time, having identified the key problem as a lack of a financial provider, promoted the solution to divorce as the simple expedient of remarriage.[9] In other words the solution was to bring in another man or, if the mother had never been married, to get her married. So the solution to an absent father in those days was seen to simply find another economic provider to put in place of the absent biological father. Moreover, family law was tolerant of the practice of changing the surnames of children to that of the new husband and also condoned the adoption of the children by the stepfather. It was generally held to be the best thing if the 'old father' was forgotten and the 'new father' was brought on board to create a *reconstituted family*. Although it was recognised that the biological father should have access to the children it was not a matter of policy concern if he did not exercise this right (although it may have been a matter of personal concern).

Within these policy debates it was, at that time, assumed that the welfare of the children would be taken care of if they remained with the person who had been the primary carer during the marriage, so long as the mother/child unit was adequately financially supported. Although there were discussions about the problem of one-parent families and delinquency, and also the relationship between divorce and delinquency, these problems were understood in relation to the loss of an authority figure in the family, or to the decline into poverty and insecurity. The welfare of the child was still not, at that time, seen in policy terms as connected to what we might now refer to as the child/father bond. The catalyst for this specific shift in the way in which welfare was conceptualised came largely from research findings that came from the USA. Central to this body of work was the research carried out by Wallerstein and Kelly[10] whose approach was psychoanalytic in orientation and based on a small clinical sample of children from divorced households. This work, which was highly contested,[11] nonetheless became very influential in the UK and shifted the focus of the policy gaze towards the newly perceived problem for children of the loss of a specific (biological) father with whom they had bonded (or needed to bond). In this new ideological context fathers became much more than economic providers, indeed they no longer needed to be economic providers to be seen as vital to the emotional and psychological welfare of children. The shift in the perception of the child's need for his/her father altered quite dramatically how divorce and post-divorce parenting was viewed. Whilst it had formerly been argued that it was better for the children for an unhappy couple to divorce, the orthodoxy reverted to the older style idea that the couple should stay together for the sake of the children.[12] Where this was impossible the next best thing became the idea of co-parenting on divorce. Thus it was argued that parents should continue to share the responsibilities of their children even though their marriage was dissolved.[13] In the context of remarriage it became unacceptable for a mother to change her children's surname to that of her new husband and the whole focus of policy in the 1990s became settled on the issue of how to retain meaningful contact between children and fathers after divorce. It was in this context that the new formulation to safeguard the welfare of children on divorce became the *co-parenting preference*.

2. *Shifting concepts of social justice*

The shifts in the concept of the welfare of the child which have been briefly identified above were accompanied by shifts in what was considered to be socially just and fair. In the nineteenth century, prior to the first wave of the Women's Movement, it was not thought at all unfair that married women had no rights in respect of their children, nor was it seen as a matter of injustice that children themselves had few civil rights. This extreme form of patriarchal power was gradually challenged and in the process new concepts of social justice emerged. Central to this development was the concept of equality but shifts in perceptions of what was fair and just did not rest on this idea alone. The idea that mothers should have the same rights as fathers in relation to children was not, for example, based on the idea of equality but on the idea of difference. Mothers were seen to have specific qualities which had no equivalence in fathers, but which deserved legal recognition in the form of legal rights.[14] In the same way rights were extended to children not because they were equal to adults but, initially at least, because they were different and required special protection.

More recently however, the gains made by the second wave of the Women's Movement have been interpreted as creating injustices. Typically it has been argued that women cannot claim equality with men on the basis of sameness whilst also demanding special rights on the basis of difference. Thus it is suggested that it is unfair for women to have equal employment rights whilst simultaneously claiming special rights in respect of their maternal roles. There has grown a sense that men have been left behind in some ways and that they are now the ones who are disadvantaged.[15] In referring to the situation of men after divorce, Beck and Beck-Gernsheim[16] argue:

> The woman has an income and she has the children ... But as men and women become more economically equal, either because the woman finds a well-paid job, or the court lays down support payments, or retirement insurance has to be shared out, *fathers become aware that they are at a disadvantage*, both naturally and legally. (emphasis in original)

A sense of what may constitute justice and injustice between the genders is therefore undergoing a degree of transformation.

In England in the 1980s one of the first men's rights groups was formed around the issue of maintenance payments to wives. This group was called Justice on Divorce and it demanded that men should no longer have to pay maintenance to their former wives. This campaign was largely successful. However, once maintenance to wives was effectively abolished it became clear that these same men were required to pay maintenance for their children who, typically, remained living with their former wives. The focus of the men's rights movement therefore changed; Families Need Fathers emerged and the goal became the shared custody of children on divorce.[17] This claim coincided with the shift in ideas about the welfare of children which also promoted the idea of co-parenting after divorce. The rights and justice claim made by fathers was therefore greatly strengthened by the coincidence of these two developments. Here there seemed to be a demand from fathers to be more involved with their children after divorce, at the same time that research was suggesting that children are disadvantaged if they lose contact with their fathers on divorce. It suddenly appeared that the welfare of children could be met by recognising that fathers were suffering an injustice and adjusting family policy accordingly.

It was the coincidence of these arguments that created pressure for new legislation and, although it would be an oversimplification to imply that they overdetermined the outcome of the Law Commission's deliberations on the shape that the new legislation should take, the Children Act does reflect these concerns to a large extent and has subsequently been implemented in a cultural climate that takes these arguments as new orthodoxies. It may therefore be useful to identify some of the core principles of the legislation and to explore how some of the main objectives were justified.

Core objectives of the Children Act 1989

It is possible to identify 4 core objectives of the private law provisions of the Act. These are:

1. to decrease hostility between the parties
2. to pursue a policy of non-intervention by the courts
3. to encourage joint parenting after divorce
4. to promote the welfare of the child

These are not listed in order of priority because the Act makes it clear that the paramount and/or first principle is the welfare of the child. However, I shall deal with them in this order because the effect of each principle is cumulative and they build towards the final goal of improving welfare.

1. Decreasing hostility

The Law Commission[18] took the view that hostility between parents could create conditions detrimental to the future welfare of the child. Based on the premise that the most important decisions that parents have to take relate to the children, the Law Commissioners felt that it was important to remove any other factors that could induce antagonism between parents. As it was felt that one of the main reasons that fathers often became hostile was the custom of awarding 'sole custody' to mothers, it was recommended that the concept of custody be abolished, thus removing a main source of conflict. The Act dispensed with the practice of awarding custody on divorce by separating parental rights and duties from spousal rights and duties. Thus whilst divorce would end the latter, it would no longer affect the former. On divorce parental rights and duties now remain the same as during marriage.

2. A policy of non-intervention

The key element of this policy was the stated preference in the Act that wherever possible, no order should be made in relation to the children. This policy stressed the idea that parents themselves should resolve their differences in relation to the children and that it was not appropriate in the normal course of events for an outside authority to do this. The preference for no orders was also linked to the idea that parents should not try to resolve their conflicts over children in court. To some extent it was hoped that courts would become redundant. This aspiration fits with the growing emphasis on mediation and with a growing dislike of the adversarial methods formerly adopted by some solicitors.

3. Encouraging co-parenting

Hoggett,[19] who was the main architect of the Act, argued that it was an experiment in joint-parenting. By this she meant that it would remove all obstacles to the continuation of a proper parental relationship on the part of both parents after divorce, as well as positively encouraging such developments. The whole ethos of the legislation stressed the importance of keeping fathers involved with their children and it rapidly overturned the idea that the primary carer should have special consideration after divorce.

4. The welfare of children

The decrease in hostility, the emphasis on letting parents make their own decisions and taking responsibility for child care decisions, and the encouragement of joint-parenting were all seen as crucial building blocks for creating a better environment for the welfare of children to flourish. Naturally the legislation recognised other elements in the process of protecting children, including requiring judges and others to take cognisance of the wishes of children themselves. Safeguards were also available where one parent might have been judged to be disregarding the interests of the children. But, arguably, the legislation has produced a situation in which a new and rather simplistic rule of thumb has emerged which is seen to safeguard the welfare of children regardless of many of the other circumstances. This rule of thumb is the orthodoxy of joint-parenting and the enforcement of contact.[20]

Whilst it is, of course, hard to argue against many of the core principles of the legislation, since few people would want divorce to be acrimonious and for children to suffer, the problem with such major law reforms is often less to do with original principles and more to do with how they are applied in practice and how they work when faced with rather complex situations. There are always unintended consequences of any reform measure, and sometimes these can even defeat the core objectives. It is vital therefore, to explore how parents are negotiating with each other under the new framework, to enquire how solicitors are putting the Act into practice, and to monitor whether the desired outcomes are starting to emerge. It is for this reason that we turned to empirical work.[21]

Negotiating parenthood: the project

We interviewed 60 parents who had divorced or separated after the implementation of the Children Act. The parents consisted of 31 women and 29 men and, although it is not easy to categorise social class, we interviewed a wide range of people from those living on benefits on housing estates to self-employed managing directors and professionals. Only two of our interviewees were coloured, an Afro-Caribbean man and an Asian woman. We interviewed the parents twice with a period of 12 to 18 months between interviews. We did this in order to avoid gathering a static picture of post-divorce parenthood and although this paper will concentrate on the first round of interviews it is worth noting that 29 of our 60 parents altered their post-divorce parenting arrangements significantly during this time. We contacted most of our parents through their solicitors but supplemented these numbers by recruiting from organisations like Gingerbread. Our sample was obviously not representative of the general population, however our sampling strategy was theoretically driven and thus designed to generate a sample that would cover a relevant range of parental circumstances and experiences rather being representative of all such circumstances.[22] We contacted solicitors in very different sorts of practices and locations in order to ensure a spread of interviewees. We also asked the solicitors to contact clients who had had harmonious divorces and not just the acrimonious or most memorable. Nonetheless, we cannot know whether the clients who responded were facing more difficulties than might be the norm. We also interviewed 37 solicitors in order to explore how the new legislation was being implemented at the grass roots level.[23]

On the basis of our first round of interviews we grouped the parents into three categories. These we called *Co-parenting*, *Custodial parenting* and *Solo parenting*. We had 10 co-parents, 35 custodial parents and 15 solo parents. It is perhaps worth explaining how we defined our categories. The distinction between these categories rested upon two key dimensions: *parental care* and *parental authority*. The first dimension focuses on the parent-child relationship and reflects the physical and emotional aspects of raising children. The second focuses on the parental relationship and is concerned with the extent of shared decision making about how a child should be raised. These two dimensions give rise to the following organisation:

Categories of parenthood: characteristics and patterns for 60 parents at time 1.

Dimensions of parenthood	Category of parenthood		time 1	
Sharing of parental care Sharing of parental authority	co-parenting		10	
Sharing of parental care No sharing of parental authority	custodial parenting		35	
No sharing of parental care No sharing of parental authority	solo parenting		15	
	n =		60	

Co-parenting is a flexible, interdependent pattern in which both parents give substantial amounts of care (requiring a re-ordering of the gendered pattern of care that commonly operates in two-parent households) and enter into a tacit co-parental contract which may include preserving the idea of the original 'family' and excluding new partners as parents. It is a demanding, unusual and fragile arrangement.

Custodial parenting, the dominant pattern within our sample, may also involve a lot of shared care, but this continues to be gendered and is delineated so that it is reconstituted in terms of 'residence' (usually for the mother) and 'contact' (usually for the father). Parental authority is vested in the mother alone who may share it with a stepfather in a 'reconstituted family' form of parenting. The parent with contact has little authority or autonomy.

Solo parenting is a minority pattern within which parental care and authority devolve to the residential parent alone (usually the mother). The other parent is disengaged from the children and from their former partner, usually because he becomes unavailable and sometimes because his behaviour prompts a rapid re-ordering as a safeguard for mothers and children.

In contrast to other typologies, which are usually constructed along the collaboration(good)/conflict(bad) axis,[24] none of our three categories was found to be more productive of consensus than any other. Conflict was evident among co-parents and collaboration among custodial parents. Thus, on the basis of our interviews we could not support the proposition that one type of post-divorce parenting is more harmonious than another. Each offered certain advantages and disadvantages. This is a point to which I shall return below.

Reflections on change

I want to suggest that we can look at how the new Act is affecting change at two levels. At one level we can focus on how processes and principles are changing and what the outcome of this might be for divorced couples and their children. At another level we can begin to speculate on what these changes may mean for gender relations more widely. We might therefore want to speculate on how the legislation complements or contradicts other social changes which are impacting upon gender relations. In what follows I want to address both levels but to do so tentatively. This is because the analysis of our own research data is not yet completed, and also because the Act itself is still relatively new and the significance of such an important change to divorce law is yet to be fully realised.

One of the most noticeable changes we found was that parents who wanted to co-parent after divorce felt that the new legislation supported their goals. They did not run into the obstacles that parents used to meet under the old Act which could not easily accommodate joint parenting.

> **Penny**: What we wanted was an arrangement where he could come and go freely and that the children didn't feel as if he was visiting. We tried to keep things as normal as possible.

This mother clearly shares the principles outlined in the Act. However, she goes on to say, referring, to her husband:

> **Penny**: He does need pushing. I've said to him several times that I didn't think he was staying long enough and I suggested them going to stay with him.

From this it becomes apparent that she needs to work on her former husband to make him into a fully participating co-parent. This is because it is often only at the point of divorce that men start to learn what is meant by engaged fathering. As Felicity says:

> Before we separated it was left to me to deal with the children. He had withdrawn a lot. When he first started visiting that's when his establishment of a relationship with the children really began. I've had to get used to having less time with them.

We can see from this remark though, that it is not only the father who has to adjust if he wants to have a full relationship with his children after divorce, mothers have to adjust too. But for some parents it is clear that the most important thing to maintain after divorce is what we might call the 'parenting project'.

> **Meg**: The other day he [former husband] said, 'We are a family,' and we try very hard for the children to understand that although we aren't partners, we don't live together any more, we are still very much to them the family. I never thought it would be possible for us to get on so well.

It is hard to imagine a clearer endorsement of the aims of the Children Act. But these idealistic statements can sometimes hide difficulties. We found that not all our co-parents could sustain this arrangement simply because it became too hard to give such a high priority to the parenting project if it meant that other important life projects had to be postponed or abandoned. Moving house, forming another relationship, or simply freeing oneself emotionally from a former spouse could become very difficult if one was deeply enmeshed in an ongoing parenting project.

> **Stella**: We're really trying to do our best for the children. Free access - they can see their dad when they want - but I'm not sure how well that will work out practically in the long term. When I move into the new house it will be a more formal arrangement. It is necessary to do that to split our relationship up. I can understand that the children need Nick, but I need to keep a distance or the whole of my life could become quite difficult.

It has to be remembered of course that co-parents were in the minority in our sample. For others the new ethos of the legislation either made no impact because both parents were happy with (or were prepared to accept) a more traditional style of post-divorce parenting, or the new ethos caused serious problems because one partner wanted to co-parent whilst the other could not accept a sharing of both child-care and parental responsibility. The following comment comes from a typical custodial parental relationship:

> **Colin**: Hilary made all the decisions. It was rigid in that there was no contact other than the set alternate weekends and I agreed that I would see them at my mum's. The arrangements were always that they would have exclusive contact with me and nobody else [i.e. not the new partner], and I never pushed it saying, 'Can I see them in the week?'

Or consider this comment from a mother who clearly feels she has both the responsibility and the authority in the parental relationship.

> **Sylvia**: It was just taken for granted that I would look after them, they'd stay with me. There was no way he was going to walk out with the four kids because he couldn't cope with them anyway. I could've walked out and left him with them but that's mother's instinct - you don't leave the kids with father - he hasn't got equal rights because he only sees them on Sunday afternoon. I used to let him come into the house but once he'd had a few drinks and started slandering and stuff and so I put the mockers on it. I said, 'Right I've been too lenient with you, off you go and you're not coming in the house again'. He waited six weeks, now he just picks them up and takes them out.

The mothers and fathers who were engaged in solo parenting often rejected the idea that the 'absent' parent should have contact with the child because they were seen as potentially harmful. They were not easily persuaded that the welfare of their child might lie in a different parenting arrangement even though they might regret the situation.

> **Bella**: From my point of view I think [my daughter] is better off as she is. She's out of the conflict. He was always very indifferent to her. He could have given her so much, it's a shame. I felt worried that I couldn't be both mother and father to her. I feel sad for her sake because she has to carry that all her life, that he's not interested.

The new Act was, as discussed above, meant to reduce conflict between couples to allow them more easily to form co-parenting arrangements. However, it is not entirely clear that this is what is happening. There are some statistical indications that there is now more conflict rather than less.[25] Ironically it may be the case that the new ethos has actually created a situation in which conflict is encouraged and is then difficult to terminate. I want to suggest that the current ethos almost gives free rein to conflict because there is a reluctance by the courts to accept anything short of joint parenting if one parent wants it. Basically it would seem that where there is pain, jealousy, bitterness and anger, the new Act allows for a free play of these hostilities and this is partly because there are no longer clear boundaries to restrain conflict. Under the old legislation, conflict over children was more or less 'out of bounds' because it was a shared assumption (whether for good or ill) that they would stay with the primary carer. But under the new ethos any father who wants to 'bargain' over the children is supported in so doing. Solicitors are no longer in a position to advise a father against fighting for the residence of the children and even where they do it is increasingly clear that fathers are less likely to listen and may simply change solicitors. Solicitors are also having to say to mothers that if the father threatens to go for residence he might get it. Thus they are acknowledging that women's bargaining position has changed. Before, she would have had the children, he would have had the money and they would fight over maintenance, but this is no longer the case. Putting it simply, he still has the money and now he has the opportunity to fight for the children too.

What we are witnessing is a major shift in the gender contract implicit both in marriage and in parenthood. Whereas Beck and Beck-Gernsheim[26] argue that men have come to see that on divorce women have both an income and the children (and thus feel disadvantaged), I would argue that in the UK the majority of married women with children still do not have an income or career prospects that are equal to men's and that they have given up their position in the labour market precisely to look after their children. This is still the basic gender contract. Men, on the other hand, retain their position in the labour market, even though they become fathers. But, in addition to this they are now in a position to 'claim' the children on divorce. Thus, whilst I would agree with Beck and Beck-Gernsheim that most men *think* that the situation they face on divorce is unfair if they want the automatic residence of their children, I would disagree with them that this is actually where the injustice lies. Clearly, as long as women give up so much to become mothers, it will be experienced as an injustice if this is simply ignored at divorce.

However, it would be naive to suggest that the old arrangements of absent or access fathers and reconstituted families could or should be resurrected as a policy goal. Typically, divorced mothers are more inclined to want their children's fathers to be more, not less, involved with them after divorce. But it does seem open to speculation, that if family law is going to insist on the correctness of co-parenting on divorce, mothers will want to insist much more rigorously on co-parenting *during* marriage as well. Yet recent research indicates that whilst men express an aspiration to do more with their children, in fact they are still largely absent parents.[27] Beck,[28] for example, argues that men are increasingly coming to value their relationships with their children but in his later work he recognises that this appears to manifest itself mostly at the point of divorce.

> Becoming a father is not difficult, but being a divorced father certainly is. At the moment when it is too late, the family personified by the child becomes the centre of all hope and concrete effort; the child is offered time and attention in a manner which during the marriage was allegedly out of the question, 'although I really would like to spend more time with him/her'. Divorce confronts the man with his own feelings as a father; he is the one to mourn for, having realised too late what liberation means, just as its objective slips away.[29]

Ongoing marriage obscures this basic gender injustice. That it to say that whilst many men and women find it quite fair for a woman to give up work, or to work part-time, when they have children, and also regard it as entirely right that a man should continue to work full-time or even extra-time, once they are divorced this no longer seems a fair contract. The problem is, however, that current family law policy seems only to recognise one element of this basic injustice. It supports the man against the woman who wants to maintain the gender contract, which seemed so appropriate during the marriage, into the post-divorce situation.[30] Modern family law cannot, it seems, even recognise that this might be a problem or a source of conflict.

Conclusions: considerations of social justice

The history of modern family law is, to a large extent, a history of the struggle to balance questions of justice with questions of welfare. Over the last century it has become less concerned with the issue of maintaining standards of Christian morality and has been disinclined to base policy on factors such as illegitimacy, adultery or other matrimonial offences. As these absolute moral rules diminished, the guidelines that emerged were based on the principles of equality (or at least equity and fairness) between men and women in marriage, and then increasingly the principle of the welfare of the child. These principles of course may compete with one another. The extent to which they could come into competition has been disguised until recently, however. This is because these two ideals could largely, *in principle*, operate in different spheres. Thus the principle of equality (or equity) could operate in the sphere of financial matters whilst the principle of the best interests of the child could operate in the area formerly known as custody and access. Although in practice all solicitors knew that it was impossible to separate these issues completely, at the level of policy and principle they were formally separated. Moreover, the growth of conciliation continued this obfuscation by allowing conciliators to focus only on children, and requiring solicitors to deal with financial matters. This separation can no longer operate in this way under the Children Act (and even less so under the Family Law Act 1996) and it has become much more obvious that the two principles are in conflict when fathers start to make larger claims in relation to children.

In balancing these two principles, family law has proclaimed that the welfare of the child is paramount and that questions of equality between parents, or of social justice between parents, are irrelevant to the more important question. This position might be less problematic if, at the same time, the new policy was neutral about styles of post-divorce parenthood. However, because it favours so strongly co-parenting, in practice it means that it 'sides' with fathers more than mothers because it wants to promote fatherhood as the antidote to potential harm.[31] In this context, claims by mothers that they cannot tolerate their former husbands are seen as contrary to the welfare of children and the harms caused by an enforced ongoing 'parenting project' are seen as far less significant than the harms caused by ongoing manipulation, hostility and/or resentment between the parents.

Under the current ethos, it seems almost improper to question whether the balance between social justice and welfare is correct. The rights of mothers or of fathers, if raised in this naked form, are seen as expressions of selfishness, whereas the welfare of children is a self-evident good. It is moreover assumed that parents should make sacrifices for their children. But the issue that needs to be addressed is whether social justice demands that there should be a limit to the degree of sacrifice to be made. For example, should a mother who has been the victim of violence be obliged to sustain a co-parenting arrangement? Is it axiomatically in the interests of child welfare that mothers are obliged to do this? These questions are increasingly being asked as a consequence of the way in which the new ethos disregards men's violent behaviour.[32] Our own research revealed a small number of cases of domestic violence even though we were not expressly looking for it. But although the numbers were small[33] they raise very important policy questions. The following quotation comes from a mother who initially wanted a co-parenting arrangement with her former partner. But he became violent shortly before she ended the relationship and his violence continued after she had left him with their pre-school son.

> **Kate**: I fear him very much. I don't fear anything else after Brian. Sometimes he accosts me in the street and as soon as it happens I always have a panic attack. I break out into a sweat immediately at the thought of it happening and I can't speak to him. I see his eyes and I can always tell from his eyes whether he has his nice personality or his nasty one. I'll see that and I'll panic because I know exactly what's going to happen next and know I'm going to have to endure it. So I'm

> going to have to live through it without dying, which would be a relief and it's that bad, it's that desperate and I'm looking round for someone to help me and I don't even see anything. My eyes are darting about, they don't focus and I'll just have to endure this until he decides to stop and I've no control over when it ends or how it ends and my only thought is 'How will I stop [my son] getting involved in this?'. I've got to run somewhere and, yes, I know he'll trip me up and kick me while I'm down but I've got to run somewhere and it's got to be somewhere where [my son] isn't.

This mother was not allowed to stop contact between her son and his father even though she reported that the child's behaviour was being seriously affected by his violence and her fear. What she found was that her idea of the welfare of her (*particular*) son, did not match with the orthodoxy of what constitutes welfare for children (*in general*) on divorce. Over time she became extremely demoralised and she found it quite impossible to sustain any new relationships or to start a new life because her former partner followed her and frightened away new friends. This case may seem extreme but it clearly demonstrates the problems that can follow from a policy which refuses to consider the relevance of any previous behaviour to future arrangements and which equates child welfare with father contact at all costs.

I want to suggest that we have gone too far in giving primacy to the welfare principle over the principle of social justice between men and women. The forward-looking, non-interventionist principles of the legislation mean that no past harms can be brought into the consideration of the future of the children. This refusal to look backwards has arisen from a desire to free people from old acrimonies and, of course, to simplify divorce proceedings which could become terminally bogged down in bickering and recriminations. It was also a part of the shift away from the dominance of Christian morality with its desire to punish certain behaviours or matrimonial offences. Few people would relish a return to the style of blame and punishment that was typical of divorce law in England and Wales in the 1950s. But we now face a different problem. Because the 'parenting project' is interminable we have to recognise that some behaviour, which may have provoked the divorce in the first place, also become inescapable. Thus the victimised wife becomes subject to on-going victimisation; she has no legitimate escape if her former husband insists on on-going contact with the children. It can be the same with other forms of cruelty and exploitation.

Attempting to reintroduce a concept of social justice does not, therefore, depend upon resurrecting an old style of punishment for past misbehaviour. Rather it involves recognising *on-going* harms from which divorce no longer provides an escape. We also need to give consideration to whether a form of joint-parenting which disregards the harm done to one parent (who is typically the residential parent) can ultimately be in the best interests of the children. These are not easy problems to resolve but they do need to be given serious consideration rather than being dismissed as out of line with the current welfare ethos, especially if we ignore the harm that a violent father can do:

> **Kate**: [Because] of Brian's behaviour, [my son] began to associate Daddy with shouting and Mummy with crying. And people I trust, like my sister who's a psychiatrist, would tell me 'Kate, you've got to stop the contact now. Don't keep putting him back'. But I felt - fathers' rights blah, blah, blah and that it was somehow wrong to do that, and that I must keep sending him back.

Kate, like a number of other mothers in our sample, could not understand why her former partner's violence was not taken seriously once she had started proceedings under the Children Act. Indeed her solicitor advised her not even to raise it as an issue because it would antagonise the other side and also the judge. Kate's experience was not unique. One mother was threatened with prison by her own solicitor if she would not allow contact and others accepted that they should not mention it. It would appear that whilst other areas of family law take domestic violence seriously, the Children Act has demoted its significance.[34] In so doing, the new legislation has significantly intervened in the broader issues of gender relationships. It refuses to attach any significance to the work of mothering and the costs that it entails for women and it seems, at present at least, to disregard the significance of men's violence to women. This may seem a controversial and rather stark way of framing some of the problems of the legislation and I acknowledge that this is something of an over simplification. I am also conscious that these outcomes may never have been anticipated or intended. However, power relations between men and women are being affected by this new ethos. On the positive side it might appear that more men are starting to take fatherhood seriously at the point of divorce (if not before) and that many mothers welcome a greater sharing of post-divorce parenthood. On the negative side, manipulative and violent men find their behaviour condoned. As one of our fathers stated:

> **Anthony**: Well, you get serial killers and rapists still have contact with the kiddies, doesn't mean to say they're a bad parent.

Perhaps one of the most worrying unintended consequences of the new law is this growing belief that there is no such thing as a bad father. In the light of such assertions it seems increasingly important to return to the thorny problem of the balance between welfare and justice in order that the positive elements of the new ethos are not overshadowed by an unthinking orthodoxy which equates mother's rights with selfish individualism and father's rights with child welfare.

Notes

1. The project, entitled 'An Investigation into the Legal and Moral Ordering of Households in Transition' (R000234582) is funded by the ESRC. I am working on this project with Dr Bren Neale at the University of Leeds.
2. Brophy, J., 'Child Care and the Growth of Power' in Brophy, J. and Smart, C. (eds), *Women in Law*, Routledge, London, 1985, who disputes that there has ever been an actual preference for mothers. Whilst I agree with her analysis - which is based on the empirical actuality that in the 1970s and 1980s the custody of children went to mothers simply because fathers did not want them and not because the Courts preferred mothers to fathers - this term does capture an ideology which was current at that time and which certainly forms a sharp contrast to the dominant ideology of shared parenthood apparent in the late 1990s.
3. Mason, M.A., *From Father's Property to Children's Rights*, Columbia University Press, New York, 1994.
4. Norton, C., *Caroline Norton's Defence*, Academy, Chicago, 1982, originally 1854.
5. Whitelegg, E., et al, *The Changing Experience of Women*, Basil Blackwell, Oxford, 1985.

6. Hopkins, E., *Childhood Transformed*, Manchester University Press, Manchester, 1994; and James, A. and Prout, A., *Constructing and Reconstructing Childhood*, The Falmer Press, Brighton, 1990.
7. Giddens, A., *The Transformation of Intimacy*, Polity Press, Cambridge, 1992.
8. Finer, M., *Report of the Committee on One Parent Families*, Vols. I and II, HMSO, London, Cmnd 5629, 1974.
9. Smart, C., *The Ties that Bind*, Routledge and Kegan Paul, London, 1994.
10. Wallerstein, J. and Kelly, J., *Surviving the Breakup*, Basic Books, New York, 1980.
11. Maccoby, E., Depner, C. and Mnookin, R., 'Co-parenting in the Second Year after Divorce', *Journal of Marriage and the Family*, 52, 1990, pp.141-155; and Furstenberg, F. and Cherlin, A., *Divided Families: What happens to Children when Parents part?*, Harvard University Press, Cambridge, Mass, 1991.
12. Richards, M., 'Post-divorce Arrangements for Children: a psychological perspective', *Journal of Social Welfare Law*, 1982, pp. 133-151 and 'Children and Parents and Divorce', in Eekelaar, J. and Sarcevic, P. (eds), *Parenthood in Modern Society: Legal and Social Issues for the Twenty-first Century*, Martinus Nijhoff, Dortrecht, 1993, pp. 307-315.
13. Roche, J., 'The Children Act: once a parent, always a parent?', *Journal of Social Welfare Law*, 5, 1991, pp. 345ff.
14. Brophy, J., 'Parental rights and children's welfare: some problems of feminists' strategy in the 1920s', *International Journal of the Sociology of Law* 10(2), 1982, pp.149-168.
15. Pahl, R., *After Success*, Polity, Cambridge, 1995.
16. Beck, U. and Beck-Gernsheim, E., *The Normal Chaos of Love*, Polity, Cambridge, 1995, at p.32.
17. Smart, C. and Sevenhuijsen, S. (eds), *Child Custody and the Politics of Gender*, Routledge, London, 1989.
18. Law Commission, *Review of Child Law: Guardianship and Custody*, Law Commission No. 172, HMSO, London, 1988.
19. Hoggett, B., 'The Children Bill: The Aim', *Family Law*, 19, 1989, pp. 217-221; and 'Joint Parenting Schemes: The English Experiment', *Journal of Child Law*, 6(1), 1994, pp. 8-12.
20. Smart, C. and Neale, B., 'Arguments against Virtue: Must Contact be enforced?', *Family Law*, 1997, p.28.
21. See note 1.

22. Mason, J., 'Decision-taking in the Fieldwork Process: Theoretical sampling and collaborative working', *Studies in Qualitative Methodology*, Vol. 2, 1990, pp. 25-50.
23. Neale, B. and Smart, C., '"Good" and "Bad" Lawyers?: Struggling in the Shadow of the New Law', *Journal of Social Welfare and Family Law*, forthcoming, 1998.
24. Categories of post divorce parenting discerned by other researchers include: harmonious co-parent, conflicted co-parent and single parent (Lund, M., 'The Non-Custodial Father: Common Challenges in Parenting after Divorce', 1987, in Lewis, C. and O'Brien, M. (eds), *Reassessing Fatherhood*, Sage, London, 1987); communicative, parallel and no contact parent (Simpson, B., McCarthy, P., Walker, J., *Being There: Fathers after Divorce*, Relate Centre for Family Studies, Newcastle, 1995); and co-parenting, parallel parenting and single parenting (Furstenberg and Cherlin, *op. cit.*). The Stanford Custody project, based on a sample of 900 Californian families, distinguished 3 patterns of co-parenting: co-operative, disengaged and conflicted (Maccoby et al, *op.cit.*; Maccoby, E. and Mnookin, R., *Dividing the Child: Social and Legal Dilemmas of Custody*, Harvard University Press, Cambridge, 1992). Our classification closely resembles that of Furstenberg and Cherlin.
25. The extent of legal dispute among parents is difficult to gauge. Statistics are per child, not per family. We know the numbers of children subject to contact and residence disputes but, since a child could be subject to both, we do not know the overall number of children who are involved in legal conflict. However, we can make conservative estimates from the available statistics.

    Table 1 shows that, despite the non-interventionist principle of the Act, between 1992 and 1995 there was a small, but steady, increase in the number of applications for both contact and residence, and a corresponding increase in the number of orders made. The number of applications for contact has increased by approximately 25%, while the resulting orders have more than doubled over the same period of time.

Table 1. Residence and Contact Proceedings in England and Wales, 1992-1995

		Applications	Orders
Residence	1992	28,060	16,424
	1993	31,214	22,232
	1994	34,252	24,050
	1995	34,751	25,390
Contact	1992	33,112	17,367
	1993	38,728	27,508
	1994	41,456	31,534
	1995	43,063	35,754

(Source: Lord Chancellor's Office: Court service)

Prior to the Children Act, the assumption was that approximately 50% of cases were uncontested, 40% of cases were negotiated in the shadow of the law, and 10% of cases involved court imposed solutions (Eekelaar, J. and Clive, E.Mc., *Custody after divorce: the disposition of custody in divorce cases in Great Britain*, Centre for Socio-legal Studies, Oxford,1977; Priest and Whybrow, 'Custody Law in Practice in Divorce and Domestic Courts', published as a supplement to the English Law Commission's Working Paper 98, *Review of Child Law - Custody*, HMSO, London, 1986). Following the Act, conservative estimates based upon the number of contact proceedings alone indicate that in 1995 approximately 20% of all children under 16 whose parents were divorced were the subject of a legal order for contact. Whilst we recognise the problems involved in extrapolating these figures, there is a suggestion here that there has been a doubling of the numbers of cases where the courts feel they need to impose a solution. **NB:** The numbers ofchildren aged under 16 who experience their parents' divorce have remained relatively stable over the period of the introduction of the Children Act (155,740 children in 1985, 148,911 children in 1987, 168,248 in 1992, 164,834 in 1994 (OPCS 1995; Haskey *op.cit*; Haskey, personal communication)).

26. See note 16.
27. Ferri, E. and Smith, K., *Parenting in the 1990s*, Family Policy Studies Centre, London, 1996.
28. Beck, U., *Risk Society: Towards a new modernity*, Sage, London, 1992.
29. Beck and Beck-Gernsheim, *op. cit.* at p. 154.
30. Smart and Neale, *op. cit.*

31. *ibid.*
32. Kaganas, F. and Piper, C., 'Domestic Violence and Divorce Mediation', *Journal of Social Welfare and Family Law*, 3, 1994, pp. 265-278; Hester, M., Humphries, J., Pearson, C. et al, 'Domestic Violence and Child Contact', 1994, in Mullender, A. and Morley, R. (eds), *Children living with domestic violence: putting man's abuse of women on the child care agenda*, Whiting and Birch, London, 1994; Radford, L., *Domestic Violence and Child Contact Arrangements in England and Denmark*, The Policy Press, University of Bristol, 1996.
33. We estimated 5 clear cases of violence against women out of our sample of 31 mothers. One also included a sexual assault, two also involved violence to children, one also involved possible sexual abuse towards a child.
34. Hester and Radford, *op. cit.*

2 Two Contemporary Problems of Family Law - of Fast Track Mothers in Custody Disputes and of the Feminisation of Poverty in Later Life

PROFESSOR ALASTAIR BISSETT-JOHNSON, Chair of Private Law, University of Dundee

Introduction

Since I started to teach Family Law in 1963 I have been struck by the way changes in demographic and other trends in society and the family, such as the changed position of married women, have left the law one step behind. A particularly interesting example is the changing position of married women. For example, whilst women, the usual instigators of divorce proceedings, almost invariably got out of marriages with which they were dissatisfied, they were all too often left to battle about their parental rights or financial matters. This had the effect of continuing the fight with the estranged partner. Sometimes the law left a spouse financially worse off where the marriage ended in death than if she 'cashed in' her marriage and asked for the return of her investment![1] The aim of this chapter is to weave together these two strands. The illustrations I have chosen are topical ones, although I readily admit that they may not represent the totality of the picture.

Professional mothers involved in custody disputes

Some history, social background and statistics

Thirty-five years ago there was thought to be a preference in custody cases for courts to award custody of young children to their mothers under what may be called the tender years or maternal preference doctrine.[2] Although the term 'residence' dispute was introduced into English law under the Children Act 1989, and was recently introduced into Scots law when Part 1 of the Children (Scotland) Act 1995 came into force,[3] most of the case law cited uses the older term and the more familiar term 'custody' disputes rather than 'residence' disputes has been retained.

It is probably true that the 'tender years/maternal preference' doctrine is now merely a make-weight factor in determining the welfare of the child in cases where the scale pans are evenly balanced. It does not have the force of a legal presumption.[4] Nevertheless references to 'motherly love' and an award of custody to a mother being 'more in accordance with nature'[5] are not uncommon in Scottish cases[6] and many practitioners still advise fathers seeking custody of young children that they face an uphill task. What is not clear is the effect of the new instruction to courts in Scotland not to make any orders relating to parenting unless '[the court] considers that it would be better for the child that the order be made than that none should be made at all'.[7] This provision mirrors the provision in s. 1(5) of the Children Act 1989, whose provisions, in the main, do not apply in Scotland. Neale and Smart have claimed that this provision may have led mothers reluctantly to agree to contact or courts to exhibit an unwillingness to make orders relating to parental responsibilities even when the situation within the family was highly conflictual and recourse to a judicial 'non-intervention' was not necessarily helpful.[8] Against this background some custodial parents make the best 'private arrangement' with their partners that they can. At the same time the Children Act 1989 has led to some men thinking the Act legitimised a new form of fatherhood which provides the fathers with increased standing in any battle for parental rights which goes to court. Smart and Neale argue that this new rhetoric of increased parental rights may have doubled the number of contested access/contact proceedings going before the English courts.

The statistics relating to what one might term the 'average case' seem to bear out preference for mothers obtaining custody, perhaps suggesting that the 'tender years' or 'maternal preference' doctrine still has some weight as a rule of common sense although judges are wise enough not to cite it as a rule of law. In Priest and Whybrow's 1986 study 'Custody Law in Practice in the Divorce and Domestic Courts'[9] it was revealed that in several studies done between 1973 and 1985 the mother was awarded custody in between 72% and 81% of cases. This appears to confirm either a judicial preference for mothers in custody disputes or a reluctance by fathers to seek custody, based either on the legal advice they received or their reluctance to undertake the job. One interesting factor post 1973 was the emergence of joint custody orders, which rose from 3.4% to 18.1% in 1985, at the same time as there was a decline in the awards of sole custody to husbands. Sole awards of custody to husbands declined from 19% to 9% in the same period. Priest and Whybrow noted the increase in joint custody at the apparent expense of husbands who would otherwise have got sole custody. But in addition to this there was a considerable regional disparity in the attitude of the various courts surveyed in the calculation of the average result. Close scrutiny of the result of the various courts working in isolation from one another revealed that three markedly different approaches to joint custody emerged:

(i) a positive promotion of joint custody;
(ii) a reluctance to interfere with the joint proposals of parents; and
(iii) a scepticism towards the concept of joint custody.

The high level of custody orders in favour of mothers may therefore represent a range of factors operating with the courts and parents:

(i) a feeling that where the mother and father's cases are evenly divided the tender years or maternal preference doctrine tips the scale pans;
(ii) the fact that most fathers have been reluctant to seek custody orders;

(iii) a feeling that in traditional families mothers have more time to parent children.

One might describe this latter feeling as representing an almost historic approach to the family. The current reality is one of a high number of working mothers and a situation in which the Government has allowed the 'married women's allowance' in tax law to wither on the vine at the same time as there has been insufficient help for non-working mothers. It is, perhaps, too early to see whether the post experience of the Children Act 1989, since it came into operation in England, has affected the historic approach of the courts.[10]

Mothers who earn as much or more than fathers

Of course, increasingly mothers are working either by choice or necessity and it is this aspect that I wish to examine, and in particular I am interested in those professional women who are mothers and who have careers which are at least as demanding as those of the fathers of their children and whose salaries reflect this fact.[11] In the U.S.A this has been recognised by some firms offering women the choice between a ' fast track' promotion, where time for family is limited, and the 'mommy track' where more time for family is expected but where the promotion prospects may be reduced. No doubt feminists would criticise the choice as either false or one which rewards women who enter the fast track by having them adopt male attitudes to careers.

The problem emerges in a very acute form for women like Marcia Clarke, the prosecutor in O.J. Simpson case, who faced an argument in a custody dispute with her husband that the welfare of her children was better served by their father having custody. He argued that he had more time to devote to his children than a busy prosecutor handling nothing but high profile cases.[12] What is in the best interest of the child of two busy working parents? The main question may merely be which parent will drop the child off at and collect the child from day-care where the child will spend most of his or her waking day. An alternative formulation might be whether it is the paternal or maternal grandparents who will look after the child while both parents are at work. I should add, however, that I am not unaware of the fact that even though men are doing more of the household chores than hitherto there is still some imbalance which is particularly evident in which parent has the major say or who undertakes the major responsibilities for child-rearing.[13]

A Canadian case involving some of these issues, *Jones v Jaworski*[14] attracted a great deal of concern from feminists in Canada. The parties were married in 1972 and separated in 1983. He was a law professor, though he moved into practice during the course of the proceedings, and she was a paediatric endocrinologist. In 1984 when the children were four and two a joint custody agreement was incorporated in the divorce. The parties were to endeavour not to alienate the children. The mother was to have the boys live with her in her home which was described as their 'ordinary residence' and they were to attend a French immersion school. There was nothing in the agreement which prohibited the mother from changing her residence to one outside Alberta, though the parents were to consult on matters involving the boys. The father was entitled to very generous access. The father remarried and had two daughters by his second wife. The boys saw a lot of their half sisters when they spent time, as they frequently did, with their father. The mother then remarried and wished to move to Ottawa to take a new position. She claimed that she was entitled to take this step unilaterally and to take the children with her. The boys' father said that she had to show that the move was compatible with the best interests of the boys and by order obtained the return of the children to Alberta to have an adjudication there.

The parties agreed on the appointment of a sole independent expert witness to interview the boys. The boys told the witness, who interviewed them at length, that they were very attached to their school and activities in Edmonton, and to their father, step-mother and half-sisters. They also resented an element of deception in the way the mother had presented the trip to Ottawa. The children had been led to believe that the move was only temporary. The boys realised that if their mother moved to Ottawa to her new job and to be with her new husband they would see less of her. However, the expert was impressed by the fact that the children's interview with him resulted in him stating:

> the most impressive sentiments, because of their spontaneity and their appearance in a number of different contexts, was the loss they would

> feel if they were removed from the Jones family in Edmonton. I was led to the strong conviction that their attachments here are very strong, and their disruption would constitute a major adjustment and even potential trauma for the boys to deal with.[15]

Given that the judge stated that the burden of proof was on the party seeking to change the residence of the children,[16] the mother had failed to meet this burden. She could keep the children if she did not move, but if she moved to Ottawa she had to relinquish care of the children to the father and to accept instead the same generous access that she had seen fit to offer her former husband. This amounted to six weeks in the summer, two thirds of the Christmas holidays, any weekends when she was in Edmonton and of which she had given the father reasonable notice. The father was to pay half the air fares for the summer and Christmas visits. The mother had been placed in the position of having to choose between her job and new husband and her children.

The decision leaves unclear what options are open to a court in cases where a parent with access (usually the father) wishes to move and the move would deprive the child of valuable contact with the parent which has furthered the child's best interests.

The principle for cases in Scotland

The decision in *Jones* v *Jaworski* suggests that if:

(i) the wishes of the child now have to be taken into account under the Children (Scotland) Act 1995, with the wishes of children over 12 being presumed mature (ss.6(1) and 11(7)); and
(ii) the welfare of the children is paramount; and
(iii) moving is stressful for children and adults, involving as it does the loss of friends and changing school;[17] and
(iv) the children can be as well looked after by the non-custodial parent who has already had a substantial involvement in the rearing of the child which will minimise any detrimental effect of a change of custody, then;

(v) the custodial parent who wishes to move to pursue their own career and personal life may have to consider losing custody of their child or children.

The worst case scenario for the parent is one in which the proposed move will deprive a child of family and friends to whom they are close, as well as having to move from a school at which they are doing well, when the other parent competing for custody is continuing to live in the area in which these ties can be maintained.

Jones v *Jaworski* can have importance in Scotland, since Part 1 of the Children (Scotland) Act 1995 is operative,[18] as s.6 requires parents or those acting in their place, when exercising any major parental decision to have regard, so far as is practical, to the wishes of the children concerned. Children of 12 and upwards are deemed to have the maturity to form a view. Younger children will have to have their maturity established and it will be interesting to see how the rules about establishing the wishes of the children emerge in the delegated legislation. One suspects that there will be less resort to expert witnesses than in Canada. Married women should be aware that the 'Super Woman'[19] who can perform superlatively at her three tasks of housekeeping, parenting and a career is something of a myth for all bar Shirley Conran. For such individuals the welfare of the mother and the welfare of her children are related but not identical. If the *Jaworski* decision is followed in Scotland successful working women in demanding jobs who are also mothers may find their increased status in society and in the work place has rebounded against them in custody battles.

Succession - does the bairn's part lead to the poverty of the mother in old age?

My second example of how changing demographic and social trends can affect the married woman arises in the field of succession. In 1995[20] it was reported that the daughters of Sir Nicholas Fairbairn had been largely disinherited by him in a will made by him earlier and amended by a codicil made only hours before his death. The daughters had apparently expected to inherit Fordells Castle subject only to a life rent made in favour of their stepmother. Fordells had, after all, been bought for Sir Nicholas by the daughters' maternal Grandmother, Lady Reay, the mother of Sir Nicholas's first wife. Instead they found that they were only entitled to a third share of Sir Nicholas's moveables including his own abstract paintings and some of his personally designed and striking apparel! The Castle was later reported to have been sold on the orders of Lady Sam Fairbairn for a sum in excess of the estate agent's asking price of £500,000.[21]

The right to disinherit children sparked a spirited debate in the Correspondence section of *The Times*[22] on the right of a father to disinherit his children with contrasts being drawn between the comparative virtues and vices of English[23] and Scottish law.[24] The Principal of the (London) Psychotherapy Centre wrote that for children to be disinherited was 'emotionally devastating for them. If we can't trust our own parents to love and want us who can we trust?' This led me to think that the current law of intestacy in Scotland might make a married women better off on divorce than under the corresponding laws of testate succession - a striking contrast with exhortations from the Law Society of Scotland to make a will. The intestacy rules permit a widow to take the matrimonial home up to £110,000,[25] furniture and plenishings of up to £20,000 plus an additional cash right of £30,000 or £50,000 according to whether or not there are children. In contrast, in cases of testate succession the home could be left to the mistress! It is uncertain why the legal rights provisions in the Succession (Scotland) Act 1964 merely restricted freedom of testation in respect of moveable property. The matrimonial home, after all, would probably be the most valuable asset at the time of the death of one of the spouses. Perhaps the limited restrictions on freedom of testation had its origin in the fact that, at the time of the 1964 Act's long gestation period, home ownership in Scotland was much less common than today. More recently the practice of couples purchasing matrimonial homes in joint names, usually with a special destination[26] in favour of the other spouse, has meant that cases in which the matrimonial home is bequeathed outside the family are relatively rare.[27]

Changing demographic trends and legal rights

The Fairbairn case prompts discussion about the merits of the claims of widows, as opposed to fit adult children, on their husband or father's estates. The *legitima portio* of Scottish children has a venerable history going back to Roman times.[28] This arose, however, under quite different social conditions with quite different morbidity conditions prevailing. If we consider the life expectancy of a Scottish man and woman in 1861 we find that it was 40.3 and 43.9 respectively.[29] If we then consider the mean age at marriage in the same year, it was 26.8 for a bachelor and 24.9 for a spinster. It follows that when the father of children died the eldest child was, in the average case, likely to be in his or her early teens and just about to make his or her way in the world. In contrast the life expectancy of a man and woman born in 1972 is 67.3 and 73.7 respectively (for those born in 1991 the figures are 71.4 and 77.1 respectively). If the mean age of somebody marrying in 1992 is 27.1 for a bachelor and 25.5 for a spinster, then one might expect that, even allowing for the later age at which women have children,[30] when the father now dies the children are likely to be in adulthood, possibly just heaving a sigh of relief at having got their own children through University and hopefully into a job.[31] Their mother would probably have at least six or seven years of life in front of her against a background in which, although more married women are working,[32] they are doing so in a context in which their earnings still lag substantially behind their male counterparts. They are also less likely to have occupational pensions, or if they do have occupational pensions, are less likely to have the same number of years of service as their male counterparts. It is no surprise that single and widowed woman are overrepresented in the two lowest quintiles of adults in the expenditure survey set out in 'Social Focus on Women'.[33] At the same time the government is using the Community Care (Residential Accommodation) Act 1992[34] to transfer many of the social costs of permanent care of senior citizens onto the persons concerned rather than meeting this cost itself as part of the National Heath Service.[35]

In short the changing morbidity figures suggest that married women now need more protection from the laws of succession than they used to and that adult children now need less protection than children 150 years or more ago when the child had a greater need for a bairn's part. Paradoxically, it is also possible to argue that legal protection afforded to a married woman by the laws of succession in Scotland were stronger than their current counterparts. The rights of *terce* and *jus relictae* enjoyed in older times were, one might argue, a better protection for widows than is provided for by the current law. 75 years ago the widow enjoyed:

(i) *terce*, a form of life rent in one third of her husband's lands of which he was infeft[36] at his death. The abolition of *terce* in the Succession Law (Scotland) Act 1964 coincided with a slow and growing increase in home ownership in Scotland which was fortified by the sale at advantageous prices of council housing to sitting tenants and a great increase in house values generally. Thus one of the most valuable assets owned by a husband is free from such a claim. It should be further pointed out that Scotland has never had anti-avoidance rules preventing the defeating of the interests of widows in their husband's heritage.[37]

(ii) *jus relictae*, the one third share in moveables that a widow was entitled to where her husband died leaving surviving children rising to a half where he did not.[38]

(iii) *community property* - at one time Scottish law flirted with the concept of community property between spouses,[39] but ultimately rejected it save for the concept of the sharing of the profits of a marriage on divorce.[40]

The exclusion of heritage from the property over which a person had no freedom of testation in 1964 when the Succession Law (Scotland) Act was passed is interesting. At the time when the Act was drafted, which was some time before it was passed, home ownership was less common than it has now become, and the sale of council houses to tenants had yet to come.[41] In practice most homes purchased today by married couples will be purchased in joint names with a special destination[42] so that the exclusion of heritage from provisions affecting freedom of testation might be thought to be of limited importance. However, investment properties and heritage bought in a mistress's name will be beyond the reach of a surviving spouse. Life insurance will often be bought under a trust which gives considerable discretion to the trustees to do the right thing by a surviving widow even if the proceeds of the policy are not part of the deceased's estate. However, given the variety of trusts, indentures and circumstances in which trustees might be called on to exercise their discretion, there is no guarantee that the widow's position will be respected in the face of claims by a mistress, a second wife or children.

Women who have married and maintained their job during their career do not face a lack of resources in their retirement years in quite the same way as the surviving widow who married at a time during which it was not merely the social convention that the family home be in the husband's name, but also the convention that the husband was expected to be the 'breadwinner' and the wife the manager of the home and nurturer of the children, a full-time job. These wives have found that the rules of the game have changed in a variety of ways since their marriage. The expectation now is that women will work and, whereas the National Health Service was expected to provide free service from the cradle to the grave, the expectation now is that much of the service formerly provided free in hospital is now provided on a means tested basis in nursing homes as part of the move to community care. If the husband is now admitted to a nursing home he will be expected to contribute to the costs of the home out of his own resources, the only significant set of resources available to support both himself and his wife. It is true that the family home will not be sold over the wife's head to defray the nursing home costs. However, the money left to the wife by way of income after a contribution to the husband's nursing home care has been deducted may be insufficient to let her live off her own resources and maintain the home in some sort of decent standard of living.[43] I should point out that currently nursing home costs can be as much as £375 p.w. and those in a senior citizens' home as much as £275 p.w. Such a wife suffers a double hardship - she may suffer a depressed standard of living during the last years of her husband's life where he is unable to live with her in the family home and, when he dies, she suffers from the estate that might have flowed through to her having been depleted by the claims of the public purse.

The rationale for the Roman law of *legitima portio* was that parents 'should not be allowed to treat their children unjustly [as where] the testator had been led astray by the blandishments or incitements of step-mothers'.[44] It was this that gave the children a claim, though at a later stage in Roman law Justinian changed the size of the *legitima portio* of a testator's children from an entitlement of a quarter to a third, where there were four or fewer surviving children, or a half where there were five or more. Some of this belief in a right of the children to an inheritance still finds its way into the attitude of Scottish people today.

Current social attitudes and law reform

The social attitude of Scots towards the surviving spouses and the bairns' right to part of their spouse's or deceased parent's estate is interesting. In an 'Attitude Survey Towards the Succession Law in Scotland',[45] conducted before the Community Care system had really begun to impinge on people's consciousness, the percentage of correspondents who thought that the children had no right to a share in their parent's estate as against their surviving parent, usually the mother, varied between 51%-65% according to whether the estate was average or poor. The percentage who favoured an equal division between the mother and the children varied between 19% and 13% according to whether the estate was of average size or was small. It seems that this attitude survey was crucial to persuading the Scottish Law Commission's decision to retain legal rights for children rather than abolishing them or restricting them to children with a claim to alimentary provision against their parents.[46]

So far as children are concerned, heritage which is left by a father to his *second* wife, and over which the children have no claim, raises an acute problem about a testator's loyalty to a second wife as opposed to his obligations to his children from a first marriage, especially where the heritage concerned was the family home of the first marriage and represented the chief profit of that marriage. The same Scottish Law Commission Attitude Survey[47] revealed much stronger support for the claims of the children as opposed to those of the wife where the surviving wife was a second one. Nor is this a local phenomenon since, in Canada, in those Provinces where the same division of matrimonial property regime applies on death as on divorce,[48] the most bitter battles have been between surviving second spouses and the children of the deceased's former marriage.[49] The length of the second marriage (in contrast to the first) is probably a crucial factor. When the Scottish Law Commission issued its 'Report on Succession'[50] the proposals on 'legal shares', the replacement term for legal rights, still seemed to be fairly conservative in the face of changing demographic trends and the shift towards minimising the cost to the public purse of care for the elderly. Under clauses 5 & 7 of the draft Bill attached to the Report, the basic scheme is to give the surviving spouse 30% of the first £200,000 of the net estate together with a claim to a further 10% in any excess over £200,000- similar rules apply to the legal shares of children where there is no surviving spouse.[51]

Take a case where the house is not in joint names and is worth £100,000. Assume that there is another £100,000 worth of assets. The widow's share is hardly adequate to provide her with a modest living. It might be argued that there will often be insurance monies paid behind a trust to help the widow and of which she will be named beneficiary and which will not form part of the deceased's estate. This may only partly be true, for the size of the insurance policy may not be great, especially if any part of policy has been used to pay funeral expenses and any mortgage still outstanding on the home. At the present time even a sum of £100,000 will be unlikely to produce an annuity of £11,000 for joint lives at age 65. Equally it might be argued that the widow may have a right to share in her deceased husband's occupational pension scheme, which, because it will exist behind a trust will also not form part of the deceased's estate. Married men should consider the sum their spouse will receive from a typical pension scheme such as the University Superannuation Scheme if they die in retirement with a pension of £15,000 p.a., and many will not even achieve this because they will either not have the requisite 40 years of service or, even if they do, the average of their best three years service will not be £30,000 p.a. If a married man dies with only 30 years service and pensionable salary of £30,000, his surviving spouse's pension will be about £5,250 p.a. plus whatever of the £45,000 tax free lump sum has been turned into a joint lives annuity policy.[52] And many pensioners will be worse off than that. In the real world it is difficult to separate out legal entitlement from the size of the entitlement.

This is exactly the sort of real life context that does not emerge from the Scottish Law Commission Paper. It is largely black letter law but with only limited acknowledgement to the amounts that people would need to live off, the average age at which people die, and similar matters.

My belief is that, if one is legislating for the usual case, and no legislation can legislate for every case, then the case for a 'bairn's part' in the present law needs review. There is a case for a 'bairn's part' in exceptional circumstances but that can be provided for by giving courts discretionary powers to deal with exceptional cases, perhaps along the line of the English Inheritance (Provision for Families and Dependants) Act 1975. If the law does not recognise the social context of the differences in which men and women live, the fact that in general married women will enjoy greater longevity, a career with service interrupted to look after children, and probably reduced resources because of that then it has not created true equality for married women.

Equally in the context of the *Jaworski* case, if women are to be encouraged to work the same long hours as men to achieve success, should they not be warned of the risks that they run if their marriage breaks down and a custody dispute ensues.

Notes

1. A classic example of this is the Government's Community Care scheme. Until April 1996, if an elderly husband had to be admitted permanently to a nursing home because his wife could no longer care for him, she could find that the whole of his occupational pension was diverted to meet her husband's nursing home costs, leaving her with no claim to his occupational pension, often the main source of family income. Although the wife was protected from having the family home sold over her head to meet her husband's nursing home costs, it did not necessarily give her an income to live in and maintain the home. In contrast if the wife divorced her husband half the pension accruing during the marriage would be hers as of right under the Family Law (Scotland) Act 1985, and in addition she would have the right to seek continuing support from her husband under s.9(1)(e) of the same Act. A less extreme solution would be for the wife to launch proceedings for aliment under the 1985 Act in the not unreasonable expectation that, if her husband's income is sufficient, the award may exceed income support level and leave some of the cost of meeting the husband's nursing home fees to fall on the taxpayer whilst bearing part of them herself as a 'liable relative'. Happily this position has changed with the National Assistance (Assessment of Resources) Regs. S.I. 1996 602 and

the wife will be able to keep half the husband's occupational pension. I am grateful to Tim Hewitt, formerly of the Tayside Social Work Department for discussing this matter with me. This dichotomy illustrates the difference between the public and private aspects of family law, a topic for another occasion.

2. Based on comments by judges such as Lord Romilly M.R. in *Austin v Austin* (1865) 34 Beav.257 at 263 in which it was said:
'Nothing .... can, in my opinion, with regard to a child of tender years, supply the place of a mother.' Christine Davies has a catalogue of cases in *Family Law in Canada*, Carwells, Toronto, 1984, p. 532 et seq. in which this doctrine was applied in Canada. Similar sentiments can be found in England as late as 1970 [*Re C(A), (An Infant)*)] 1970 1 W.L.R. 288 at 289, though the principle in both England and Canada is now treated, not so much as a presumption of law, as a deciding factor where the welfare of the child would be equally well served whichever parent obtained custody. The position in Scotland seems similar to that in England. In *Hannah v Hannah* [1971] S.L.T.(N) 42 at 43 when the Lord Ordinary awarded custody to a mother on the basis that such a course was 'more in accordance with nature', even though this resulted in a daughter being taken from her father and his girl-friend with whom she had lived for several years. The Lord Ordinary's decision was reversed for concentrating on matters other than the welfare of the child, which in the instant case, was better served by the preservation of the status quo. The matter has recently come to the fore in the Inner House decision of the Court of Session in *Brixey v Lynas* [1996] S.L.T. 908, noted [1997] *Family Law* 10.

3. Initially only a few sections of the Children (Scotland) Act 1995 were brought into force under the Children (Scotland) Act 1995 (Commencement No 1) Order S.I. 1995/2787. The remainder of Part 1 of the Act and most other sections were brought into force by the Children (Scotland) Act (Commencement No 2 & Transitional Provisions) Order S.I 1996 2203 with effect from November 1st 1996 or by the Children (Scotland) Act 1995 (Commencement) No.3 Order 1996 3201 from April 1997.

4. See *Brixey v Lynas* [1996] S.L.T. 908.

5. *Hannah v Hannah ibid*, though the Inner House reversed the Lord Ordinary for relying on those words. More recently Lord Morrison is quoted in *The Scotsman*, June 13th 1996, in an unreported case as suggesting 'that during infancy Scottish courts are inclined to recognise a child's stronger need for a mother'.

6. See Thomson, J., *Family Law in Scotland*, Butterworths, Edinburgh (3rd edn), 1991, p. 226.
7. See Children (Scotland) Act 1995 s.11(7)(a).
8. See Neale, B. and Smart, C., 'Arguments against virtue - must contact be enforced?', *Family Law*, 1997, p. 332 and '"Good" and "Bad" Lawyers?: Struggling in the shadow of the law', *Journal of Social Welfare and Family Law* (in press).
9. Published as a supplement to the English Law Commission's Working Paper 96, *Review of Child Law - Custody*, HMSO, London, 1986.
10. For a study of the early experience see Neale, B. and Smart, C., 'Arguments against virtue', *supra*.
11. This is, it must be admitted, a relatively small percentage of cases. *Social Focus on Women*, HMSO, London, 1995, p. 33, Table 2.26 estimates the percentage of women earning more than their partner at 13%, usually comprising younger women in non-manual employment.
12. See *The Times*, March 10th 1995. Ms. Clark's estranged husband alleged in a Los Angeles court in which he was demanding primary custody of their two sons aged five and three that: 'on most nights she does not arrive home until 10.00 p.m. and even when she is at home she is working'. He alleged that he, an engineer, was at home most nights by 6.00 p.m. and could spend his evenings with the boys. Ms. Clark's salary of approximately $100,000 p.a. was alleged to be double that of her husband. Ms. Clark's supporters claimed that women were being held to a double standard in which they were encouraged to pursue high flying careers but then penalised in custody proceedings if they did so.
13. See *Social Trends*, 1995 (vol. 25), Table 2.7. This reveals that between 1983 and 1991 the percentage of couples who equally share the shopping had only gone up from 44% to 47%, and those who share the evening meal making has only gone up from 17% to 20%. When it comes to looking after sick children, this was predominantly a woman's job in 1993 (63%) and remained so in 1991 (60%). Interestingly, a much higher percentage of couples thought cooking and shopping should be shared (76% in both cases).
14. (1989) 18 R.F.L (3d) 385(Alta Q.B).
15. *ibid*, at p. 395.
16. *ibid* at p. 394: 'because it was the unilateral decision of *Jaworski* to make such a move, the onus should be placed upon her to satisfy the court that such a change would be in the best interests of the two boys

rather than the usual onus resting with Jones'. More recently in *Goertz v Gordon* (1996) 134 D.L.R. (4th) 321 the majority of the Supreme Court of Canada was prepared to consider imposing restrictions on the custodial mother, a dentist, when she sought to travel to Australia to undertake further studies in orthodontics. The father's objection was that such a move would involve a disruption in the frequent and meaningful contact that he was having with his daughter. The Supreme Court of Canada held that in variation proceedings such as these, the father had to meet a threshold test of showing that a material change of circumstances had occurred. A relocation by the custodial parent that had the effect of disrupting frequent and meaningful contact between the child and the access parent met that test. Thereafter the judge had to embark on a fresh inquiry as to where the best interests of the child lay. In doing so the circumstances in which the original order was made and any new circumstances had to be reviewed. In this inquiry there was, contrary to the minority position of L'Heureux-Dubé, J. *et al*, no legal presumption in favour of the custodial parent, though their views were entitled to great respect. The reasons for the move of the custodial parent were generally irrelevant save where they disclosed an improper motive. The Divorce Act of Canada in ss.16(10) and 17(9) required a judge to keep in mind that generally it was in the interest of the child to have maximum contact with both parents. The importance of the child remaining with the parent with existing custody in a new location had to be set against the continuance of contact with the access parent, extended family and its community. Ultimately the mother was allowed to retain custody of the child because of the length of time the child had been in the custody of the mother and the likelihood of severe disruption to the child if custody were changed. Fortuitously for the mother, the child did not object to the move and the means of the father allowed him to travel to Australia to exercise access there and this could be supplemented by an order permitting him to have access to his daughter in Canada.

In contrast L'Heureux-Dubé and La Forest would have assumed that the existing custody order should continue, and the custodial parent retained the right to determine where the child was to live unless the non custodial parent could satisfy the burden of proving that the change was detrimental to the best interests of the child. In those exceptional cases where the parties had agreed, or a court order stipulated, that the child's residence should not be changed without the permission of the other parent the burden of proof that a change of residence was in the child's best interest rested on the custodial parent. Such an approach strengthens the position of the custodial parent and may avoid the expense of litigation to them.

17. Stress tables indicate that moving is a significant stressful event in an adult's life, though clearly less so than death or divorce. See Holmes, J.H., and Rahl, R.H., 'The Social Readjustment Rating Scale', *Journal of Psychosomatic Research* (11), 1967, pp. 213-218. Children's priorities may be different from those of adults. For children the effect of moving may be even more significant. Studies suggest that if the reason for a child moving can be seen as affecting the child's self esteem, such as changing households, or where the move was over 150 miles or deprives it of its support systems, then adverse effects, often significant, on the child may be discerned. See Warren-Sohlberg, L. and Jason, L., 'How the reason for a school move relates to school adjustment', 29(1), *Psychology in the Schools*, 1992, pp.78-84, and Munton, A.G., 'Job Relocation, Stress and the Family', *Journal of Organizational Behaviour*, 11(5), 1990, pp. 401-406.
18. See Children (Scotland) Act 1995 (Commencement No 2 & Transitional Provisions) Order 1996 S.I. 2203.
19. Conran, S., *Superwoman - every woman's book of household management*, Sidgwick & Jackson, London, 1975.
20. *The Times*, July 12th and 15th, 1995.
21. See *The Scotsman*, November 11th, 1996.
22. See *inter alia*, *The Times*, 'Daughters seek legal advice on Fairbairn will', July 12th and 15th, 1995.
23. Until quite recently a testator in England could leave all his property to the Battersea Dogs' Home rather than his wife and children. However the position was changed when the Inheritance (Family Provision) legislation was introduced into English law from New Zealand in 1937. This legislation enables statutorily defined dependants who feel that no proper provision has been made for them to apply to the court to make proper provision for them by either rewriting the testator's will, or by applying the laws of intestacy so that proper provision is made for them. The testator is allowed to indicate, in letters or other means separate from the will, the reason why no provision is being made for the dependent. The cost of such proceedings usually falls on the deceased's estate and can make for very bitter intra-family litigation. The current legislation is the Inheritance (Provision for Families and Dependents) Act 1975. The dependants who can invoke the legislation include:
(a) the spouse of the deceased;

(b) the ex-spouse of the deceased if not re-married;
(c) a child of the deceased;
(d) a person who, though not a child of the deceased, had been treated by the deceased as a child of the family by the deceased;
(e) any person not previously covered who, immediately prior to the death of the deceased, was being wholly or partly maintained by the deceased. (The so called 'mistresses charter'.)
In order to prevent a spouse who has lived with their partner until death-do-them part being worse off than one who divorced their partner, 'reasonable financial provision' for a spouse is to be measured against what would have been likely to have arisen in divorce proceedings (s.1 (2)(a)). Although the conduct of the dependant is relevant to the testator's decision to cut them off without proper provision there is some doubt about whether the conduct of a surviving spouse should be differently viewed than in financial provision on divorce where it is generally disregarded unless 'obvious and gross'. In *Re Snoek deceased* (1983), *Family Law* 13 18, Wood, J. declined to hold that the actions of a wife who hit her terminally ill husband with a rolling pin and a milkbottle, punctured the tyre of his car, threw water over him as well as writing abusive correspondence to his business colleagues was sufficient to justify him in making no provision for her at all. She had contributed to a 20 year marriage and raised the children and was entitled to something for that. It will be noted that adult children have a *spes successionis* rather than a right of inheritance and therefore have an uphill battle to establish that no proper provision has been made for them, especially if the bulk of the estate has been left by the deceased to the surviving spouse.

24. In contrast to English law, Scottish law has for centuries made provision for relicts and bairns. The current Succession (Scotland) Act 1964, following the common law, restricts a testator's freedom of testation by providing a surviving spouse with a *legitima portio* of one third of the deceased's moveable estate if there are children, and a half of the moveable estate where there are no children. Children, by parity of reasoning, have a half claim to deceased's parent's moveable estate if there is no surviving spouse and one third if there is. At one time there was believed to be a *communio bonorum* under Scottish Law by which the first spouse to die could leave their share of the community property by will. See the discussion of *Lashley v Hogg* (1804), 4 Paton 581 in the first edition of Anton, A.E., *Private international Law*, W. Green &

Son, Edinburgh, 1967, p. 456, but this rule was later relegated to the role of a legal fiction.

25. Or £110,000 if it exceeds that value. The Prior Rights of Surviving Spouse (Scotland) Order S.I. 1993/2690. In fact if the home is bought in joint names without a special destination a house of £220,000 value could pass to the surviving spouse under the laws of intestacy. Such a value would cover all but a very few homes in Aberdeen, Edinburgh and Glasgow and even a few country estates.
26. A form of will substitute in which property is usually left to the surviving spouse.
27. Manners, A.J. and Rauta, I., found in *Family Property in Scotland*, HMSO, London, 1981, that 37% of matrimonial homes were owner occupied and, of those bought in 1977, 78% were bought in joint names. The percentage of owner occupied houses and those bought in joint names since 1977 has probably gone up.
28. Borkowski, A., *Textbook on Roman Law*, Blackstone Press, 1994, pp. 230-232; Thomas, J.A.C., *A Textbook on Roman Law*, North Holland, Amsterdam, 1976, p. 495.
29. All figures,unless otherwise stated, are taken from Scottish Office, *Scottish Abstract of Statistics*, 1992, Vol. 21 10.
30. See *Social Focus on Women*, C.S.O., 1995, p.16, which suggests that the average age at which women are having a first baby is now 28 and their are more women having their babies in their 30s and 20s.
31. This point was recognised by the Scottish Law Commission in its *Report on Succession* (Report 124), 1990, para. 3.8, but ultimately did not persuade the Commission to depart from the existing scheme which a majority of individual correspondents had favoured and which had the virtue of certainty.
32. *Social Focus on Women*, C.S.O., 1995, ch.2, suggests that the proportion of women who were economically active was now 44% compared with 37% 20 years ago. However, the greatest increase was in part-time low paid jobs.
33. *Social Focus on Women*, C.S.O., 1995, 55, Table 3.1.
34. See also the National Health Service & Community Care Act 1990 implementing the Government White Paper, *Caring for People* (Cm 849), HMSO, London, 1989.
35. Since the 1995 Budget it is probably widely known that anybody with assets of over £16,000 (formerly £8,000) does not qualify at all for Community care, and that those with assets of £10,000-16,000 are required to make some contribution. Equally well known is the fact

that, though the matrimonial home will not be sold over the head of a fit spouse whose partner needs residential care (currently around £275 p.w. in the private sector) or nursing care (currently round £375 p.w. in the private sector), the charge will accumulate against the property until paid off. Not so well known is the fact that if the partner needing care is a husband with an occupational pension, the main asset of the family to fund retirement, and the wife does not have an occupational pension, then the whole of the pension is available to meet the husband's care costs. (See The National Assistance (Assessment of Resources) Regulations 1992, S.I. 2977; 1993, S.I. 964 & 2230; 1994 S.I. 825 & 2386; 1995 S.I. 858 & 3054.) The sum left to the wife may be inadequate for her to maintain and heat the matrimonial home since she will be treated as a single person with no claim to the pension and have to rely on income support. It is true that Reg. 5. of S.I. 2977 gives the Local Authority a discretion to increase the pocket money/personal allowance of the person in care and this might increase the sum available for the wife but most local authorities are reluctant to use this power since it would have the effect of increasing the cost of care falling on local authorities and diminishing the cost of income support to be met by central government. In keeping with the logic of the Pension Act 1995 the position of the wife has been changed from April 1st 1996 by 1996 S.I. 602 to enable the wife to treat half the income from her husband's pension as her own property. The question of division of the tax free capital sums derived from a pension is not yet clear. If the Local Authority believes that the wife has too much to live off and can be expected to contribute to her husband's costs of care as a 'liable relative' then she may be asked to contribute to it. One might speculate whether at some point the wife would be better to ask for a divorce and for the division of matrimonial assets under ss. 9-17 of the Family Law (Scotland) Act 1995 in an attempt to be left with a more favourable financial position than under the funds left to her under the National Assistance (Assessment of Resources) Regs. One might suspect that this drastic remedy might be confined to the cases where the husband's mental state might prevent him from appreciating that he had been divorced - e.g. a case of dementia. This is another example of the public and private aspects of family law being out of step - a topic for a paper in its own right. *The Times*, November 29th, 1995 suggests that the government is investigating allowing the elderly to shelter more than £16,000 from the sum required to meet the costs of their care where they plan ahead for such costs or by changing the tax rules so that people can opt for a lower pension soon after retirement with the sum rising as the risk of residential care increases. Neither plan is likely to help any but a small section of retired people. This is particularly true where a local authority has a higher than average number of pensioners resident in its area and its limited resources make it difficult to honour the financial limits stated in the delegated legislation. In such circumstances the decisions in *R v Gloucester Country Council (ex parte Barry)* [1997] T.L.R. 146 and *Reg. v Sefton Metropolitan Borough Council* [1997] T.L.R. 165 suggest that although the resources of the local authority might be relevant, albeit to a limited extent, in determining whether an elderly person was in need of care, the Court of Appeal has recently held (*Regina* v. *Sefton Metropolitan Council,* Times Law Report Aug. 23 1997) that once the local authority had determined that a person was in need of care, it had a duty to provide that care. Its lack of resources was no excuse. Nor was it open to the local authority to use its lack of resources to depart from the National Assistance (Assessment of Resources) Regulations 1992 (SI 2977) which required assistance to persons in need of care with less than capital of £16,000.

36. See Gloag, W.Mc. and Henderson, R.C., *The Law of Scotland,* 1st edn, W. Green & Son, Edinburgh, 1928, p. 449. The need for infeftment (symbolic possession) prior to the Conveyancing (Scotland) Act 1924 meant that lands purchased by a husband but without his having taken infeftment were free from terce whereas lands sold by a husband but prior to the purchaser taking possession were subject to it. Certain subjects could not be the subject of terce, including leases, superiorities and feu duties.
37. See Scottish Law Commission Consultative Memorandum No. 69, *Intestate Succession and Legal Rights*, 1986, p. 212.
38. For more detail see Gloag & Henderson, *op. cit.*, p. 451ff.
39. See the discussion in *Lashley v Hogg* (1804), 4 Paton 581 discussed in detail in Anton, *op. cit.,* p.456. For further reading see Gardner, J.C., *Origin & Nature of the Legal Rights of Spouses and Children*, 1928, in the Scottish Law of Succession, W. Green & Son, Edinburgh; Carey-Miller, D.L., 'Rights of the Surviving Spouse', *Acta Juridica* 49, 1980; Anton, A.E., 'The Effect of Marriage on Property in Scots Common law', 19 M.L.R., 1956, p. 653; Meston, M.C., 'Matrimonial Property in Scotland', *Jur. Rev.*, 1970, p.193.
40. See the Family Law (Scotland) Act 1985 especially ss. 9(1)(a) and 10(4).

41. The majority view seems to have been that not only did the abolition of *terce* and courtesy remove an unnecessary and difficult administrative burden on heritable estate, but that:
'in small estates where there was little cash and the house and the furniture are the main assets, the widow scoops the pool... with a larger estate the balance between the widow and the children will be even worse' (per Lord Guest H.L Debates, Vol 250, 1963/4, p.579). The Earl of Perth's comments seem to have been to similar effect, namely, that the most likely victims of the Bill were the children of the deceased rather than the surviving spouse.
It was left to Lord Reid (H.L. Debates, Vol 250, 1963/4 at p. 590/91) to point out the difference between the provisions governing testacy and intestacy. He said:
' ...on intestacy the widow is extremely well off, but if a will is made (in favour, for example, of a mistress) she may be quite badly off. She does not get the house, she does not get any other provisions: she gets no legal rights out of the heritage ... all she gets is legal rights out of the moveable part of the estate. That is not much.'
42. In the survey conducted for the Scottish Law Commission, *Family Property in Scotland* (H.M.S.O., 1981), Manners A.J. and Rauta, I. found that 37% of all matrimonial homes in Scotland were owner occupied (Table 2.1). For homes purchased after 1977, 78% were owner occupied, a rise from 57% for those bought prior to 1977. The percentage bought in joint names will probably have risen since 1977.
43. Liquid assets over £16,000 will be available to meet the husband's nursing home expenses under the National Assistance (Assessment of Resources) Regulations. Until recently the same Regulations (see note 1) even denied the wife a share to her husband's occupational pension which could be totally used to meet the expenses of maintaining him in a residential home or nursing home, forcing the wife to live off income support or other means tested benefits. The fact that the situation changed from April 1996 cannot disguise the extent to which the private and public aspects of family law are often out of step.
44. Borkowski, *op.cit.*, p. 230, citing the Digest 5.2.4.
45. Printed as Appendix 2 to Scottish Law Commission Consultation Paper 69 on *Intestate Succession & Legal Right*, 1986.
46. See the Scottish Law Commission, *Report on Succession*, No.124, para. 3.10. 60% of the individual respondents to the Attitude Survey conducted by the Commission favoured a *legitima portio* for children.

Many of the institutional consultees such as the Scottish Landowners Federation, the National Farmers Union, and Committee of the Scottish Clearing Bankers opposed it (para. 3.8). The Law Society of Scotland seemed initially to favour legitim but in later comments appeared to favour discretionary provision (at 18 note 1).

47. *op. cit.*, p.228.
48. See for example Nova Scotia and Newfoundland.
49. See for example *Mills v Andrews* (1982) 142 D.L.R. (3) 294 (N.S.S.C.T.D.), *Re Levy* (1981) 131 D.L.R. 15 (N.S.C.C.T.D.), *Sagar v Bradley* (1984) 10 D.L.R. (4th) 565 (N.S.C.A.).
50. Scottish Law Commission Report 124, January 1990.
51. Where there is a surviving spouse then the children's share is (i) halved and (ii) they cannot claim against the first £100,000 of net estate of which the spouse inherits the fee (as opposed to a life rent) under the deceased spouse's will or the laws of intestacy. This aims at reversing the decision in *Kerr* Pet. 1968 S.L.T. (Sh. Ct.) 61 discussed by Macdonald, D.R., *Succession*, W. Green & Son, Edinburgh (2nd edn.), 1994, at p.260.
52. See the example in the USS Handbook at p. 17.

3 'Come out and fight like a woman': Gender Differences in Violent Behaviour

PROFESSOR GERDA SIANN, Chair of Gender Relations, University of Dundee

Introduction

> It pays males to be aggressive hasty, fickle and indiscriminating....It is more profitable for females to be coy.[1]

That women commit fewer crimes than men and that, when they do commit crimes the crimes are far less likely to involve violence, is seldom regarded as open to question. In this paper I want to explore the evidence for this perceived gender difference and then to look at a number of theoretical approaches to gender differences in aggression and violence. At the outset, however, I would like to make clear that in discussing violence I am focusing on violence to the person and am not including references to violent acts directed towards property.

Violence in human beings has traditionally been linked by social scientists to the notion of aggression, with aggression being regarded as the prime emotional precursor of violence. But obtaining agreement on the definition of human aggression has been fraught with difficulty, chiefly because some theorists of aggression regard it as a potentially positive emotion which may be subverted under particular circumstances into a negative and destructive force whereas others define aggression as inevitably negative in nature. Proponents of the first view, that aggression is a potentially healthy emotion, may for example cite the case of a woman who has been dominated by her partner psychologically for a long period and who turns to a therapist for help. The therapist may suggest that it is more constructive for her to respond in a challenging and aggressive, even violent manner to him than to turn her anger inwards and become depressed.[2] On the other hand it has been argued by other theorists that aggressive behaviour is underpinned by the desire to injure others and is inevitably destructive.[3] I will be taking this dichotomy into account in my discussion of the differing perspectives on the aetiology of gender differences in aggression and violence.

But before embarking on a description of these perspectives I would like to consider the evidence for gender differences in violent behaviour. In the first instance, as indicated above, women commit fewer crimes, particularly serious crimes, than men (for example, recent British figures show that 7% of the female population will have had a conviction for a serious offence by the age of 31, compared with 33% of males[4]). Looking specifically at violent crimes, Heidensohn, reviewing British, European and American figures in 1996, concluded that women's share of violent offences has remained relatively stable for a number of years at about 11%.[5]

Other commentators, however, argue that there is some evidence that in recent years gender differences in the area of violent behaviour are beginning to diminish particularly in the case of younger women involved in street/gang violence.[6] At the same time, a number of studies have begun to document the fact that women as well as men report behaving violently towards their partners[7] though there is no doubt that within heterosexual relationships men are far more likely to inflict serious injury than women. In general, then, it seems fair to conclude that while men continue to behave more violently than women, as rigid differences in sex roles are beginning to diminish, the identification of physical violence solely with men is also diminishing.[8]

As an example of this, I would like to cite the anecdote which lies behind the subtitle of this chapter. One hot summer day I was idly watching a group of children playing with water pistols. As one of the girls dived for cover, I heard a boy challenge her to come out of her hiding place by calling: 'Come out and fight like a woman', revealing, I thought, two things: - first that he accepted that girls fight, and second that they fight differently from boys. But when I asked him why he had challenged her in that particular way, demonstrating an impeccable sense of political correctness, he said 'Well she's a girl so you've got to say it like that'.

Leaving my misinterpretation of his remark aside, my initial reaction to what he said revealed two salient aspects of my own thinking about gender differences and violent behaviour: (i) that there is an increasing social acceptance that violence can be part of the repertoire of behaviour of females as well as males, but that (ii) female violence is seen as different in kind to male violence.

That women are more likely than they were in the past to be seen to be overtly involved in violent behaviour seems to me not to be in dispute. On the one hand, in the area of what I term 'legitimised violence', in many western countries women have moved into occupational spheres, which were previously the preserve of males, such as the police and the armed forces, where they are expected to take part in physically violent interactions. And on the other hand, in the area of what might be termed 'illegitimate' violence public attention frequently focuses on individual cases of female violence, for example, in the seventies and eighties on the female members of terrorist movements, such as Patty Hurst in the USA and Ulrike Meinhof in Germany, and more recently on female serial killers such as Myra Hindley and Rosemary West, and women involved in street violence, such as the young women who were convicted of assaulting Liz Hurley.

It is important, however, to note that the media focus on women involved in violence rests in many ways on sex role stereotypes in that while male violence is presented as a normative and expected component of masculinity, female violence is nearly always presented as emerging from some form of psychological disturbance. Thus, while in the media men are frequently represented as violent because of their social background as in the presentation of football violence as emerging from a 'lager lout' culture, women who are violent tend to be presented as being mentally ill. Similarly within the criminal justice system, reports on female offenders are more likely to stress psychological pathologies than reports on male offenders. For example, in one study it was found that there were twice as many statements referring to the offenders' psychological processes in the case of reports on females.[9] The message is the same, women are seen as more likely to be involved in violent behaviour now than they were in the past but those that are so involved are seen as different from violent males.

The belief that violence is a normative aspect of male rather than female social behaviour, though widely held, rests on number of different perspectives on human aggression and violence and I turn now to five of the most influential of these accounts, considering them particularly in the context of gender differences.

The biomedical perspective

The history of criminology has always reflected a comforting tendency on behalf of the law-abiding majority to come to terms with the criminal, and particularly the violent criminal, by locating the causes of their inequities in biological and constitutional factors. This tendency is comforting because such an explanation saves the non-criminal observer not only from examining the law breaker's environment for any factors which might have caused him or her to behave in so seemingly unintelligible a manner, but also from taking any action to change such an environment.

Casare Lombrosa, while not the first person to suggest that criminals were 'degenerate' at a physiological level, was the first person to undertake a systematic effort to study biological factors in criminal behaviour.[10] In 1876 he suggested that the characteristics of primitive men and inferior animals periodically reappeared in certain individuals who, in fact, revealed the 'stigmata of degeneration' - certain characteristics of the head and skull, lobeless ears, small and receding chins and facial asymmetries.

While no contemporary criminologist would endorse so simplistic and crude a doctrine, Lombrosa's perspective is reflected in contemporary terms by those who claim that violent behaviour is largely, if not entirely, caused by physiological pathologies. The pathologies that have been cited are many and varied and include genetic disorders - for example chromosomal abnormalities and specific genes for violent behaviour; brain abnormalities such as tumours in the limbic system, imbalances in neural transmitters, specific types of epilepsy and head injuries; abnormalities in the autonomic nervous system; hypoglycaemia; hormonal imbalances, and the action of drugs and chemicals such as alcohol and food additives.[11]

Adherents of the biological approach to violence are not particularly interested in the emotional concomitants of violent behaviour. Consequently they have little to say about aggression and never examine the issue, referred to in the introductory section of this paper, which is that aggression may potentially be positive and constructive. Their approach is essentially reductionist because they de-emphasise the importance of human emotions regarding human beings as essentially biological organisms who are reducible to physical systems. Arguing that violence is intimately related to physiological abnormalities they also believe that such behaviour can be modified by physical intervention. At the individual level they frequently advocate physical solutions such as castration (surgical or chemical) and psychosurgery for violent recidivists. In some cases they have even moved beyond the individual case to advocate mass screening for biological defects.[12]

Most of the work on the biological basis of violence has been linked to the investigation of male criminals, particularly in studies which have linked violent behaviour to high levels of male hormones such as testosterone, to men with XYY chromosomes and to men such as boxers who have suffered repeated brain injuries. In general, biological theorists tend to discuss violence in the context of male offenders with a relatively strong emphasis on the linkage between masculine hormones and violent behaviour. There are some exceptions to this bias however.

The first relates to the early work of Lombrosa who with Ferrero attempted to extrapolate their identification of physiological degeneracies in criminal men to women, concluding that criminal women were essentially masculine in appearance.[13] These early speculations received little subsequent attention and in the following century attention to female criminality tended to fix on women who offended against the prevailing codes of morality, particularly sexual morality, rather than on those who committed crimes of violence.

More recently, as biologically inclined theorists have focused on the link between testosterone and male violence, attention has also been turned to a link between pre-menstrual changes in levels of hormones and crimes of violence. This focus has been utilised successfully by defence lawyers in a number of well publicised cases in the last decade, notably in the trials of Christine English who crushed her former lover against a telegraph pole with her car, and Sandra Craddock who was charged with killing a fellow barmaid.[14]

In general, however, those who regard violence as essentially due to physiological pathologies, have tended to take for granted that such pathologies are more characteristic of males than females. This applies not only to sex-linked pathologies such as the XYY chromosomal abnormality but also to other pathologies, for example abnormalities of the limbic system, which are not sex-linked. It is likely, however, that in future the linkage between female hormones and violence may continue to be made and the use of PMT as a defence for violent acts may increase. But it is somewhat ironic that when it comes to the link between women's biology and violence it is the association of their hormonal levels with violent criminality that is emphasised rather than the association between their relative lack of physical strength and male violence.[15]

Essentialist perspectives

The belief that violent behaviour is underpinned by physiological pathology is, of course, determinist in nature. The assumption is that an individual's physiology predisposes him, and far less frequently her, to criminality and violence. A similarly determinist perspective on violence is found in what have been termed 'essentialist' perspectives. These perspectives, and I shall be discussing two of them in this section, locate the propensity for aggression and violence in human nature particularly in masculinity.

Socio-biological approaches

Socio-biologists are concerned with the application of evolutionary theory to social conduct, seeking to explain social conduct by relating it to concepts of genetic advantage and biological fitness. While most socio-biologists do acknowledge the role of learning and culture they consider their influence to be very limited, arguing that most human behaviour has its roots in evolutionary mechanisms such as the personal survival of the individual and the reproduction of the group.

For many,[16] though not all, socio-biologists, aggression is one of the chief mechanisms contributing to individual and group welfare. In this view they echo the tradition of earlier generations of ethologists like Konrad Lorenz, who in defining aggression as 'the fighting instinct in beast and man which is directed against members of the same species' claimed that 'aggression, far from being the diabolical, destructive principle....is really an essential part of the life-preserving organisation of the instincts'.[17]

In short, according to Lorenz, man is by nature aggressive, aggression is potentially positive and it is properly characteristic of males rather than females. He reserved total contempt for non-conforming males:

> but there is an expression, taken from animal behaviour, for the contemptible really submissive man: he is called henpecked, a metaphor

> that well illustrates the abnormality of male submissiveness, for a real cock does not let himself be pecked by any hen, even his favourite.[18]

Lorenz's views that aggression is a natural and healthy characteristic of males rather than females and needs to be discharged, have found ready public acceptance and have been echoed both in popular books (such as those, for example, of Desmond Morris) and by film makers. Indeed Lorenz's theories provided an explicit rationalisation for the directors of some of the very violent films of the seventies and eighties. For example, Sam Peckinpah, who directed the notoriously violent *Straw Dogs* in which the heroine is portrayed as becoming fascinated against her will by aggressive men of action and who as a result betrays her timid and withdrawn husband, publicly acknowledged his debt to Lorenz's theories.[19]

Lorenz's perspectives were developed by socio-biologists, such as E.O. Wilson, who argue that sex differences in the propensity to aggression and violence are rooted in an evolutionary past in which men were the hunters and women the primary caretakers of infants and children.[20] Under such circumstances they believe particular and different traits came to be innately determined in males and females. For example, they note that female ova are scarcer than male sperm. They argue that this difference has given larger, stronger and more aggressive males an advantage in reproducing because they are more able than their weaker peers to mate with many women hence optimising their chances of having offspring. Thus, according to socio-biologists, there were evolutionary pressures for men to be more adventurous and aggressive and as a result, even today, men are essentially more aggressive and violent than women.

As might be expected the views of ethologists and socio-biologists which downplay the effect of the social environment have been very critically received by many social scientists.[21] They have also attracted a great deal of adverse attention from some feminist writers for the same reasons.[22] Other feminist writers, however, take up a somewhat similar socio-biological stance to that of Wilson. Adrienne Rich, for example, agrees with Wilson that there are essential differences determined by evolution between the sexes but focuses on women's sense of co-operativenesss and empathy rather than on male aggression.[23]

Socio-biological accounts of gender differences have been termed 'essentialist' in that they rest on the belief that females and males are *essentially* different in nature. In this belief and in their emphasis on aggression as quintessentially masculine rather than feminine, socio-biological perspectives on gender differences and aggression are very similar to psychoanalytic views and it is to these that I now turn.

Psychoanalytic approaches

The term psychoanalytic approaches is used to cover a wide gamut of approaches that derive from the seminal work of Sigmund Freud but there is some degree of consistency in the approach to gender differences, which are located for most psychoanalysts[24] chiefly in the dynamics of the early years and in particular in the relationship with the parent of the opposite sex. During these early years, and particularly during what has been termed the 'Oedipal stage', psychoanalysts claim that gender differences develop from the differing ways in which infant boys and girls relate to the parents of both sexes. With specific reference to aggression. Freud argued that boys identify with the active masculinity of the father. Girls, on the other hand, aware that they will never be able to identify with their father's masculinity, because of their physiological dissimilarity, form a desire for passive intercourse with a sexually aggressive father.

Thus Freud argued that, as a result of the dynamics of the Oedipal stage, gender differences, in general, pivot on the active/passive dimension and that intertwined with the active pole of this dichotomy is the merging of activity with a relatively benign form of aggression. He also believed, however, that the active/passive dichotomy was to some extent genetically determined, noting that 'the accomplishment of the aim of biology has been entrusted to the aggressiveness of men', and that consequently women are more passive because their active involvement is not necessary for the procreation of children.[25]

Although there is some variation in the manner in which psychoanalysts discuss gender differences in aggression,[26] the great majority of psychoanalysts echo three of Freud's assumptions. First, - aggression is an inescapable characteristic of human nature with positive as well as negative implications. Second, that gender differences in aggression are located in the essential and innate nature of masculinity and femininity. Third, these differences are amplified by the dynamics of early family life. In addition they tend to agree on another underlying assumption, which is by no means confined to psychoanalysis. This is that satisfactory heterosexual relationships involve an important element of aggressiveness in male sexuality and of yielding and submission in female sexuality. Consequently they tend to believe that women are attracted by aggressive, powerful males. However, as I have just noted, it is not only psychoanalysts who suggest that there is an innate predisposition in both sexes for men to dominate sexually and for women to seek such domination. For as Roth puts it:

> the belief that aggressiveness and power are inseparably intertwined with sexual desirability and success in the male has been handed down through the ages in many, but not all cultures, and is fostered and reinforced from many sources.[27]

There is no doubt that these essentialist beliefs about gender differences, sexuality and aggression have influenced judicial processes. First, in rape cases, it may be assumed that aggressive masculine sexuality is an inescapable absolute. For example in 1990, Harold Cassell took early retirement from the judiciary as a result of his comments when he sentenced a man to probation for unlawful intercourse with his 12 year old step-daughter during his wife's pregnancy because, according to the judge, it was understandable for a man with a healthy sexual appetite to be driven to such behaviour if his wife lost interest in sex.[28]

Second, the judiciary may treat differently women who are seen to deviate from the stereotype of the non-aggressive female. While it is regarded as acceptable, and indeed natural for men to be sexually active and adventurous, the same behaviour in women tends to be heavily censured as is evidenced in the manner in which a women's sexual past has been held up to scrutiny if she is a complainant in a rape case.[29] Further, as I mentioned in the introductory section of this paper, when men behave violently it is seen as contextually based, but when women behave violently it is seen as emerging from their individual pathology.

These essentialist themes are in fact ubiquitous in western culture and the polarity between an active aggressive, yet compelling, masculinity and an essentially passive and complimentary femininity permeate literature from the eighteenth century novels of Samuel Richardson to contemporary novelists such as Norman Mailer and Ian McEwan.[30] This polarity is, of course, also reflected in mainstream films such as *Fatal Attraction* and *Disclosure* and, in its least benign form, underpins the work of writers such as de Sade and George Bataille[31] and sadomasochistic pornography. But in recent years, essentialist views of gender differences in aggression and violence have been increasingly challenged, not only in alternative theoretical approaches, but also in mainstream culture by writers such as Sarah Peretsky,[32] by television programmes such as *Prime Suspect* and by feature films like *Thelma and Louise*.

Social perspectives

The three approaches to gender differences in aggression and violence discussed above are all determinist in that they argue that such differences rest on physiological differences, innate predispositions and the unconscious processes forged inescapably in early infancy. Such determinism can be contrasted with approaches which seek to relate gender differences in aggression and violence to social processes and the cultural environment. The further implication is that such gender differences are modifiable by social and cultural change.

The following sections review two such perspectives. The first of these rests primarily on socialisation processes while the second explores the issue of gender differences in aggression and violence within their political and cultural contexts.

Socialisation approaches

> ... many of the values of the masculine mystique, such as toughness, dominance, repression of empathy, extreme competitiveness, play a major role in criminal and domestic violence[33]

Social learning approaches to gender differences in aggression and violence rest on a model of aggression and violent behaviour as originating not in human nature but rather as provoked or induced by environmental contingencies.[34] The assumption is that aggressive behaviour is a learned mode of reacting to the social environment and aggression is defined by theorists working from this perspective as essentially negative. Their approach which was developed largely in the sixties is based on the experimental methodology which was characteristic of the psychology of that period and which derived from the empiricist perspectives of behaviourists and drive theorists.[35]

In essence, because they regard aggressive behaviour as a learned repertoire of behavioural acts or scripts which are evoked by the social environment, social learning theorists concentrate on how such behavioural scripts are acquired, what provokes them and what maintains them. With specific reference to aggression, they believe that aggressive behaviour tends to be learned by imitation in the family and social environment and by modelling behaviour observed in the social environment or on the media. They believe that it is evoked by social contexts, such as gun clubs, and that it is maintained by the ubiquity of violence in the media.

Social learning theorists have carried out an immense number of laboratory and field studies focusing on the media, particularly television and feature films, as a powerful instigator, and model of aggressive and violent behaviour particularly in children. Indeed the mass media themselves, particularly the tabloid press, frequently invoke the role of television and videos in individual acts of violence, for example in their coverage of the Jamie Bolger case.[36]

Theorists operating from the social learning perspective in both the USA and the UK have long been associated with campaigns aimed at reducing violence in the media arguing that such a reduction would be bound to reduce the level of social violence. It should be noted, however, that the majority of social scientists reject this view of the causal and pivotal role of the media in instigating and maintaining violence as overly simplistic.[37]

With respect to gender differences in aggression and violence, social learning theorists tend to argue that, while experimental studies show minimal gender differences in the extent to which women feel aggressive and express verbal aggression,[38] there are clear gender differences in the extent to which such aggression manifests itself in violence. They ascribe these differences primarily to the acquisition of gender roles arguing that current child rearing practices contribute to rewarding macho values of toughness and aggression in boys and that educational establishments and the media further reinforce and amplify these messages. From this viewpoint, it might be expected that as gender role stereotyping on the media decreases and with the advent of feature films which explore the nature of contemporary violence in contexts which show women as involved in it as men (for example *Natural Born Killers*) gender differences in violent behaviour will inevitably diminish significantly.

Social constructionist approaches

In recent years, traditional approaches to social science, such as social learning theory, have been subject to serious criticism by theorists operating from a number of different perspectives, for example phenomenology, feminism, post-structuralism and social constructionism, but who nevertheless all offer the same fundamental critiques.[39] Basically, these critics challenge the assumption of traditional social scientists that social science can operate from an 'objective' or value free position. These critics also question the methodologies that have been used in traditional social science and especially in psychology arguing that, in their attempt to be 'scientific', traditional social scientists have placed undue emphasis on large scale surveys and laboratory experiments. In so doing, these critics contend traditional social scientists have ignored the most potent sources of understanding individuals in society - people's own accounts of their actions.

Such critics also contend that traditional social science has been dominated by the presumptions, and frequently the biases, of those groups who have privileged access to power and resources. In the case of western societies such privileges have tended to be the prerogative of white middle class males. With specific reference to the area of violence and aggression, it is argued that traditional social scientists have tended not to question the use of violence by say, the police or armed forces, legitimising such violence largely without question. Critics operating from a criminological standpoint, including David Box and myself[40] have further argued that crimes involving violence are also committed by people in positions of power and privilege but that such crimes, for example when deaths occur by negligence in large companies, tend neither to be publicised by the media nor taken up by criminologists. In short, we argue that criminal law categories are ideological constructs. Further we suggest that whether or not a particular act of aggression is regarded as positive or negative, is essentially a subjective judgement on behalf of the person or persons making the judgement. Such judgements are frequently biased by their values and ideologies.

The extent to which ideology implicitly biases social categories has been taken up particularly by feminists working from what they term a 'social constructionist' perspective.[41] Focusing particularly on gender, they argue that traditional social scientists ignore the extent to which gender operates at individual, interpersonal and cultural levels to structure people's lives. Consequently, they point to the extent to which criminological studies have until recently been dominated by male theorists who have never questioned the extent to which their own gender and class position might bias their conclusions.[42] They also point out that female offenders should be viewed in relation to the complex and concealed forms of oppression and social control to which women are subject.[43] Violent female offenders have tended to be regarded as doubly deviant for breaking social rules by offending and sex roles by behaving violently.

Female criminologists in general, but particularly those working from a social constructionist perspective, have also questioned the extent to which traditional criminologists have relied on large scale studies and surveys which offer little insight into the criminal's, and particularly, the female criminal's perspective. Consequently they have tended to conduct their own research by means of in depth studies of female offenders. In this way they have illuminated the social pressures which lead to the decisions taken by such offenders. For example, in the book *Criminal Women*,[44] five female criminologists demonstrate the extent to which offenders consciously engage in crime. Similarly in her book on girls in gangs, Anne Campbell[45] argues that when an individual decides to join a gang, whether they are male or female, the decision should be viewed in the social context of inner city deprivation rather than as evidence of personal pathology.

Their position with respect to gender differences in behaviour is complex. In general, social constructionists criticise traditional social scientists for ascribing gender differences in behaviour to *fixed* gender differences in personal attributes rather than to the *social context* in which the behaviour is taking place. They argue, for example, that an individual woman may well be assertive and indeed aggressive in situations where she is operating as an equal. However, in social and occupational situations where she lacks power in comparison to the males present, she may behave less assertively because, in the circumstances, it is more effective for her to use persuasion than assertion.

Criminologists working within the social constructionist perspective also take up an issue referred to earlier in this paper which is that violent women tend to be pathologised in comparison to violent men. Whereas the actions of violent men are seen as emerging from the social context in which the deeds take place, the actions of violent women are seen largely as emerging from their status as victims or because they are mentally ill. These theorists acknowledge, however, that such pathologising may actually benefit female offenders in that, if women who commit violent acts are seen either as passive victims or as mentally ill, their sentences may be lower than if they are seen have actively taken a decision so to act.

From the perspective of social constructionism, it might be assumed that such theorists would anticipate that as sex role stereotyping becomes less marked, gender differences in violence might be expected to diminish as women become more similar in their social behaviour to men. This is a viewpoint taken up by Anne Campbell but a number of criminologists working from an overtly feminist stance distance themselves from such a view.[46] In doing so they criticise in particular, the 'sisters in crime' hypothesis put forward by Freda Adler in the seventies in the USA, which argued that as women break into a man's world, they will explicitly ally themselves with the violent aspects of masculinity.[47]

Conclusions

That women commit fewer crimes of violence than men is indisputable, although whether or not this gender difference is diminishing is disputed. The five perspectives on aggression and violence that have been discussed in this paper all offer differing explanations of these gender differences. They also differ in that, from the point of view of the first three discussed, such gender differences in violence can be expected to remain stable but from the perspective of the final two it might be expected that as gender differences in general social behaviour tend to diminish, so gender differences in violent crimes should also be become less marked.

Notes

1. Wilson, E.O., *Sociobiology: The New Synthesis*, Harvard University Press, Cambridge, MA, 1978.
2. For an example of this view of aggression see May, R., *Power and Innocence: A Search for the Sources of Violence*, Fontana, London, 1976.
3. Bandura, A., *Aggression: A Social Learning Analysis*, Prentice Hall, New Jersey, 1973.
4. Home Office, *Gender and the Criminal Justice System*, HMSO, London, 1992.
5. Heidensohn, F., *Women & Crime* (2nd ed), MacMillan, London, 1996.
6. Campbell, A., *Girls in the Gang, 2nd ed.*, Blackwell, Oxford, 1991.
7. White, J.W. and Koss, M.P., 'Courtship Violence: Incidence in a National Survey of Higher Education Students', *Violence and Victims*, vol 6, 1991, pp. 247-256.
8. Siann, G., *Gender, Sex and Sexuality: Contemporary Psychological Perspectives*, Taylor & Francis, London, 1994.
9. Allen, H., 'Rendering them Harmless: The Professional Portrayal of Women Charged with Serious Crime', in P.Carlen and A. Worrall. (eds), *Gender, Crime and Justice*, Open University, Milton Keynes, 1987.
10. Lombrosa, C., *L'Uomo Delinquente*, Bocca, Turin, 1876.
11. Siann, G., *Accounting for Aggression: Perspectives on Aggression and Violence*, Allen & Unwin, London, 1985.
12. See Clare, A., *Psychiatry in Dissent* (2nd ed), Tavistock, London, 1980.
13. Lombrosa, C. and Ferrero, W., *The Female Offender*, Peter Owen, London, originally 1895. See Brown, B., 'Women and Crime: The Dark Figures of Criminology', in N. Naffine (ed), *Gender, Crime and Feminism*, Dartmouth, Aldershot, 1995.
14. Kennedy, H., *Eve was Framed: Women and Criminal Justice*, Vantage, London, 1993.
15. *Ibid*, pp. 104-5.
16. See Hinde, R.A., *The Biological Bases of Human Behaviour*, McGraw-Hill, New York, 1974.
17. Lorenz, K., *On Aggression*, Methuen, London, 1966, p. ix and p. 39.
18. *Ibid*, pp. 109-110.
19. See Montagu, A., *The Nature of Human Aggression*, OUP, Oxford, 1978.
20. Wilson, *supra*.
21. e.g. Fausto-Sterling, A., *Myths of Gender: Biological Theories about Men and Women* (2nd ed), Basic Books, New York, 1992.
22. e.g. Birke. L., *Women, Feminism and Biology: The Feminist Challenge*, Wheatsheaf, Brighton, 1986.

23. Rich, A., *Of Woman Born*, Norton, New York, 1979.
24. Siann (1994), *supra*.
25. Quoted in Rohrbaugh, J., *Women: Psychology's Puzzle*, Sphere, London, 1981, p.125.
26. Siann (1985), *ibid*.
27. Roth, M., 'Pornography and Society: a Psychiatric View', in M.Yaffe and E.C.Nelson (eds), *The Influence of Pornography on Behaviour*, Academic Press, London, 1982, p. 13.
28. Kennedy, *supra*.
29. *Ibid*.
30. Richardson, S., *Pamela*, reprinted by Penguin, 1980; Mailer, N., *The Deer Park*, Paladin, London, 1991; McEwan, I., *The Comfort of Strangers*, Picador, London, 1981.
31. e.g. Bataille, G., *Eroticism Death and Sensuality*, City Lights, San Francisco, 1986; de Sade, D.A., *120 Days of Sodom*, Hutchinson, London, 1989.
32. e.g. Paretsky, S., *Indemnity*, Penguin, London, 1987.
33. Miedzan, M., *Boys will be Boys: Breaking the Links between Masculinity and Violence*, Virago, London, 1992, p.xxiii.
34. Bandura, *supra*.
35. Siann (1985), *supra*.
36. For a readable, if polemical, summary of this position see Medved, M., *Hollywood vs America*, Harper-Collins, Glasgow, 1993.
37. Cumberbatch, G. and Howitt, D., *A Measure of Uncertainty*, Libbey, London, 1989.
38. White, J.W. and Kowalski. J.M., 'Deconstructing the Myth of the Nonaggressive Woman', *Psychology of Woman Quarterly*, vol. 18, 1994, pp. 387-508.
39. Siann (1985), *supra*.
40. Box, S., *Power, Crime and Mystification*, 1983, Tavistock and Siann, London (1985), *supra*.
41. Crawford, M., *Talking Difference: On Gender and Language*, Sage, London, 1995.
42. Naffine, *supra*.
43. Smart, C., *Women, Crime and Criminology. A Feminist Critique*, Routledge and Kegan Paul, London, 1976.
44. Heidersohn, *supra*.
45. Carlen, P. (ed), *Criminal Women: Autobiographical Accounts*, Polity, London, 1985.

46. Brown, B. (1995), in Naffine, *supra*.
47. Adler, F., *Sisters in Crime*, McGraw-Hill, New York, 1979.

4 Gender and Sentencing

DR NEIL HUTTON, Law School, University of Strathclyde*

Introduction

The growth of feminist criminology over the last twenty years has opened up many areas of inquiry. One such area focuses on the way in which women offenders are sentenced by the courts and in particular whether this reveals systematic differences between the sentencing of women and men. This essay reviews research which tries to find out whether there are gender differences in sentencing patterns. Do women get treated differently from men? Does this difference manifest itself in more lenient or more severe sentences? Whatever the answers to these empirical questions, there remains a policy question: should men and women be treated equally for sentencing purposes or are there circumstances where gender is an appropriate factor to take into account in sentencing? This in turn raises the broader political question of whether, in general, women should receive from the law equal treatment or special treatment.

Disparity in sentencing

Underpinning these questions there stands a particular conception of sentencing. Liberal ideals of justice demand consistency in sentencing. Consistency requires that similar cases receive similar treatment. Disparity is a 'problem' because one of the central principles of sentencing is equal treatment, the idea that similar cases should receive similar punishment. The key question therefore concerns how 'similarity' is to be defined. The 'just desert' approach to punishment argues that punishment ought to be proportionate to the seriousness of the offence.[1] This is a narrow definition of similarity based on offence characteristics to the exclusion of offender characteristics and other factors which are not held to affect the seriousness of the offence. Under a strict desert approach, therefore, women offenders ought to be treated in the same way as male offenders who have been convicted of a particular offence.[2] However a closer examination of the concept of seriousness in desert theory suggests that matters are more complex. Seriousness comprises the extent of harm caused added to the culpability of the offender. Thus if it could be shown that women, in general, are more or less culpable than men for a particular type of offence, then gender may have a bearing on the calculation of offence seriousness. Otherwise, from a desert perspective, gender is irrelevant.

This emphasis on the importance of consistency in sentencing is only part of the story. This principle exists in tension with a quite different approach which argues that the choice of a just sentence depends on taking into account all the relevant facts and circumstances of the case. This is sometimes described as an individualised approach to sentencing and is the story which judges most frequently tell when they are asked to describe the process of sentencing.[3] The tension is not between consistency and inconsistency but between different ways of defining what counts as a similar case. The desert approach provides a relatively narrow definition based on offence characteristics, the individualised approach leaves the definition of similarity entirely to the discretion of individual judges.

Thus while the concept of disparity is not incompatible with an individualised approach to sentencing, it would be impossible to measure the extent of any disparity because there are a multitude of criteria for defining similarity and there is no rational and systematic procedure specifying how these criteria are to be applied.[4] It is in this sense that sentencing is often described as 'an art rather than a science'. A desert perspective provides a clear definition of seriousness which, in principle, allows researchers to examine whether, for similar offences, women receive systematically different sentences than men. Most research into gender differences in sentencing operates with the assumptions of a desert approach. It would perhaps be more accurate to say that this research privileges a desert based definition of similarity over an individualised definition.

Many of the reforms of sentencing which have taken place over the last twenty years or so can be seen as attempts to institutionalise the desert based definition of consistency.[5] The numerical guidelines introduced in many jurisdictions in the United States all have a desert basis in so far as the penalties (either suggested or prescribed depending on the jurisdiction) are related to some definition of offence seriousness. In England and Wales, the

Criminal Justice Act 1991 makes proportionality of punishment the primary rationale for sentencing, although it is not clear what impact this has had on sentencing practice, and subsequent legislation may have shifted the emphasis away from 'desert'.[6] The Scandinavian reforms were also based on the principle of desert. In all of these examples, desert was seen as the best means of pursuing greater consistency in sentencing.

Both research attempting to uncover disparity in sentencing and legislative reforms designed to reduce disparity in sentencing have been based on a desert definition of consistency. Desert provides a convenient methodological tool for defining what counts as a similar case to allow a similar penalty to be selected. It is possible to produce a list of offences graded in a hierarchy of seriousness and this fits with an important principle of sentencing, shared by both philosophical and 'common-sense' approaches, that 'like cases should be treated alike'. However desert is not the only appropriate definition of consistency. In practice, desert alone does not provide an adequate account of how sentencers go about their job. We know from their own accounts of sentencing that sentencers deal with 'whole cases', that they take into account all the facts and circumstances of the case. There has been little research into the processes of decision-making by sentencers. (An obvious reason for this has been the difficulty of getting access for research.) Tata has argued that sentencing can usefully be compared to a range of other legal and administrative decisions where the decision-maker has a very large amount of relevant information which can be taken into account and few rules specifying how the information should be taken into account.[7] Essentially this involves comparing new cases with 'familiar' or 'typical' cases. Thus a sentencer may think in terms of 'a run of the mill housebreaking by a drug user' or 'a particularly distressing case of systematic child abuse by a stepfather' rather than thinking in terms of the facts and circumstances of the case as they are set out in the charge sheets. This is a different approach to the pursuit of consistency from that specified by the desert approach and it will produce a different definition of disparity.

Thus one of the main difficulties in the research on gender disparities in sentencing is establishing a definition of the 'normal' sentence from which disparity can be measured. This difficulty is not restricted to gender disparities, it has to be addressed by research examining any kind of disparity in sentencing.[8] While this essay focuses on the research into gender disparity in sentencing, it also questions the basis of all disparity research.

Disparity and justice

From a liberal perspective, the problem with disparity is that it is evidence of injustice. Sentencing is supposed to be just. As Hudson notes, there is an important difference between disparity and discrimination.[9] Disparity refers to 'the consistency with which criteria are applied to cases' while discrimination 'refers to the legitimacy of the criteria'. Thus if agreed criteria are applied in a consistent manner, disparity should not arise. However, discrimination can occur because of values inherent in the criteria. For example, the *Federal Sentencing Guidelines* specify higher penalties for crack cocaine than for powder cocaine. If the criteria are applied consistently then crack offenders will receive higher penalties than powder cocaine offenders.[10] From a liberal perspective, this does not constitute disparity because the criteria are applied consistently. However, as crack cocaine is the drug of choice for black users and powder cocaine is used predominantly by white users, consistent application of the guidelines produces systematic discrimination along racial lines. Black drug offenders receive much higher sentences than white drug users and many would argue that this is unjust.[11] The criteria themselves express value judgements about the relative seriousness of two types of drug offending.

This analogy can be extended to the desert approach generally. The approach treats offender characteristics as irrelevant for sentencing purposes. All offenders are to be treated as if they were the same. In practice of course they are not the same, nor are they perceived to be so by sentencers.

> The 'equality' of legal subjects is a myth; what is reality (sic) is their social and material differences.[12]

If this is true, then it will be impossible to design a set of sentencing guidelines that is universally equitable. Any guidelines will favour some sections of the offender population and will also work against the interests of those favoured by the preceding regime. Thus, for example, if the US Sentencing Commission decided to remove the discrimination produced by the guidelines on drug sentencing described above, they could either reduce the penalties for crack, increase the penalties for powder cocaine or split the difference. Whichever approach is adopted some offenders will be relatively better off than they were before and some offenders will be relatively worse off.

Is it then impossible to achieve justice in sentencing? In principle, one should discover all of the factors which affect culpability, allocate weighting according to their social distribution and calculate a score for each individual case. Hudson argues that it would be 'impractical' to calculate the 'blameworthiness' of offenders because of the large range of different pressures to which different offenders are subject.[13] This would indeed be impractical, and it would arguably get us no nearer absolute 'justice' in sentencing. Hudson's approach is essentially the same as that taken by *Sentencing Guidelines*. The difference is that the criteria are different. Hudson's criteria would be based on a calculus of factors (social, economic, family, educational, etc.) held to affect offender culpability. The *Sentencing Guidelines* criteria are based on factors affecting offence seriousness. Let us call Hudson's approach 'social justice' as distinct from the 'legal justice' promised by a desert approach. Under social justice criteria, an offender may receive mitigation because of poor educational attainment, unemployment, abusive father, etc. and receive a lesser sentence than an employed offender with educational qualifications and no history of family violence. This approach may avoid disparity so long as the criteria are applied consistently but cannot avoid discrimination against the latter type of offender. No approach to sentencing can avoid discrimination.[14] Justice is neither absolute nor essential. We need to devise procedures to achieve justice and these will always be the product of political struggle and will always be underpinned by a particular set of values.

The remainder of this essay examines the research into gender disparity in sentencing. Most of this work has assumed a desert approach to dealing with the problem of similarity. However desert is only one approach to this problem and there are other ways of defining a just approach to sentencing. The question is not whether women should get special treatment or equal treatment as all sentencing is a form of special treatment. We need to look at the effects on women offenders of a desert approach to sentencing and ask whether these are desirable according to whatever clearly articulated set of values we wish to promote.

Research into gender disparity in sentencing

One of the main difficulties in comparing the sentencing of men and women lies in the disproportionate numbers involved. There are far fewer women than men convicted in the courts. There are also significant differences in the pattern of offending between men and women. Women commit far less crime than men. There is some evidence that the proportion of women convicted of offences is growing, for example, the percentage of females among convicted offenders in US District Courts rose from 7.0 in 1963 to 10.8 in 1979.

Females represent 16.4% of offenders sentenced under the *Federal Sentencing Guidelines* in 1992. Heidensohn notes that for most Western jurisdictions the proportion of women dealt with by the criminal justice system is just under twenty per cent.[15] The pattern of women's offending is also different from the male pattern. Although women commit the same range of offences, their crime tends to be less serious, and they are less involved in professional property offending and armed robbery. In both Scotland and England and Wales, there are far fewer women than men in prison. Thirty men for every one women on average in England and Wales during the 1980s and a similar proportion for Scotland.[16]

Thus women arguably constitute much less of a problem for the criminal justice system than men. However, the existence of gender discrimination in sentencing would cause problems for the system. Apart from the 'injustice' to the affected offenders, the public perception of systematic gender discrimination could lead to a loss of confidence in the system.

As discussed in the introduction, in trying to locate gender differences in sentencing, it is important to ensure that like is being compared with like. That is, it is important to ensure that 'similar' cases are being compared where the only significant difference is the gender of the offender. The definition of 'similarity' is crucial. The two single best predictors of sentence severity found in the sentencing research literature are seriousness of offence and criminal record. Offence seriousness is the primary criteria used by the desert approach and criminal history is usually added to this as a measure of seriousness in systems of sentencing guidelines. These have also been widely used in research into sentencing disparity as a means of 'controlling' for case seriousness to allow systematic forms of disparity to be investigated.

Early research into gender disparity showed that women were treated more leniently at sentencing. However, this has been criticised for failing to take into account prior record and offence seriousness with sufficient subtlety.[17] Those studies with fewest controls tended to report large gender effects whereas those with more adequate controls find small, if any, gender effects.[18] Once offence seriousness and previous convictions are taken into account, much, but not all, of the apparent gender difference disappears. For example, in an early UK study, Farrington and Morris found that women were treated more leniently but that this could mostly be explained by their lesser criminal records.[19]

More recent research has taken more care to control for offence seriousness and has reported a small but significant degree of leniency extended to women offenders at sentencing. A review of studies in the US by Simon and Landis concluded that adult female offenders received more favourable sentences than similarly situated male offenders (i.e. those with similar records convicted of similar offences).[20] Nagel and Hagan conducted large scale properly controlled studies, one for white collar offences the other for all offences, and found evidence of preferential treatment of women at sentencing.[21] A recent review of research by Steffensmeier, Kramer and Streifel[22] argued that:

> ... a fairly persistent finding has been that adult female defendants are treated more leniently than adult male defendants... the studies substantiate the widely held belief that female defendants receive more lenient treatment (apparently) because of judicial paternalism, the social costs to children and families of sending women to prison, or the view that female defendants are less dangerous and more amenable to rehabilitation than male defendants.

The conclusions from this literature appear to support the view that women receive preferential treatment in sentencing. Criminal history and offence seriousness remain the best predictors of sentencing severity, but when these are controlled, women appear to receive slightly more lenient treatment from sentencers.

Explanations for disparity

The quantitative data seem fairly convincing, and the next problem is to try to explain this systematic leniency which appears to be exercised in favour of women. One explanation has been described as the 'chivalry hypothesis'. This argues that judges, who are predominantly male, exercise a systematic leniency in favour of women because women are held to be less responsible for their crimes or more susceptible to treatment rather than punishment. While qualitative evidence based on interviews and observation provide some support for this thesis, it also shows that matters are more complex. Some women are treated more leniently, but some are treated more harshly. Perhaps the most important conclusion from the qualitative research is that differences are due to sentencers' perceptions of conventional gender roles and the extent to which women offenders conform to these rather than to any uniform chivalry extended to all women.

Allen showed that violent women offenders received more sympathetic and individualised treatment from sentencers for serious crimes for which men got no comparable understanding.[23] Walklate's comments on this work suggest that men are more frequently ascribed responsibility for their criminal conduct than women who are seen as passive.[24] Things happen to women and they are less frequently held responsible for their actions. Thus women are twice as likely as men to be given some form of psychiatric disposal by the court. Men who murder are more likely to be represented as responsible monsters.

Worral found that women who would not allow their offending behaviour to be explained in domestic, sexual or pathological terms caused problems for the criminal justice system.[25] If they insisted on accepting responsibility for their crime (i.e. agency) and resisted treatment or management they upset the conventional representations of women operated by justice workers from magistrates to social workers.

Eaton found that both men and women conforming to conventional roles were better treated than those with unconventional lives.[26] She found that women were expected to take more responsibility for homemaking and domestic morality, a conclusion supported by Carlen.[27] Carlen interviewed fifteen Scottish sheriffs all of whom expressed their reluctance to send women to prison. When they did it was either because the woman was a bad mother, outside 'conventional family life' or because sheriffs believed that the prison could provide appropriate treatment, training or even a stable environment. Eaton found that judges said that they would take family responsibilities into consideration regardless of the gender of the offender.[28] However, in practice a greater proportion of women are likely to have child rearing responsibilities, and to be perceived to have primary responsibility by judges even if there is a male partner, so what appears to be a gender neutral decision reproduces conventional discourse locating a woman's role in the family. Thus as Walklate points out, even though men and women may be treated equally in terms of their roles in a 'conventional' family, since these roles are inequitable the court in fact reproduces the inequality of gender roles within the family.[29]

Daly called this approach 'familial paternalism'.[30] She found that defendants with families are rewarded for conforming to the norms of social adulthood and that sentencers feel that the social costs of punishing offenders with families are higher than the costs of punishing offenders without families. Thus sentencers say that they try to keep a man in employment and a woman at home with her children. Daly argues that what may appear to be leniency exercised in favour of women is in fact leniency in favour of offenders in conventional families. This appears to benefit women disproportionately for a number of reasons: (1) Women are more likely to have dependent children; (2) Familied women are perceived as fulfilling their familial obligations more responsibly than familied men; and (3) Child care is more important than breadwinning in the maintenance of families.[31] Thus, for Daly, paternalism is not for the protection of women but for the protection of the family. Familial paternalism is a response to both men and women, but child care work (typically performed by women) is prioritised over breadwinning (typically done by men). Further support for the 'familial paternalism' comes from the work of Frazier, Bock and Henretta in the US, who found that Social Enquiry Reports reproduced the same views of women's domestic role and non-criminal natures and were more likely to recommend non-custodial sentences for women (where offence seriousness and criminal record were controlled).[32]

Thus quantitative research suggests that women are treated slightly more leniently than men in similar cases. Qualitative research suggests that this apparent statistical regularity may conceal a more complex picture. Some women may indeed receive more lenient treatment but this is because sentencers perceive women as primary care givers within the family and the leniency is for the benefit of the family (i.e. children). Other women who do not conform to conventional stereotypes of femininity may receive harsher sentences precisely because they are not located in a family. There may also be cases where the 'chivalry' explanation holds (i.e. where sentencers treat women leniently because they perceive them to be less responsible, more susceptible to a rehabilitative sanction, or otherwise unsuitable for imprisonment). However the 'chivalry' explanation cannot be applied across the board to all women offenders.

It appears that there are gender differences in sentencing although they are not as significant nor as simple as early research suggested. Whether or not these differences are justifiable will be considered in a later section of the essay.

Post-guidelines research into sentencing and gender

The aims of the *Federal Sentencing Guidelines* which were implemented by the United States Sentencing Commission in 1987 were to remove unwarranted disparities in sentencing by placing substantial restrictions on judicial discretion. Sentencers have to follow a complicated and lengthy set of procedures to find the appropriate guideline sentence for a particular case.

There are certain factors which sentencers may take into account in deciding to depart from the guideline sentence. These are known as warranted departures and the factors may include age, physical condition, mental or emotional condition, family and community ties but *only* when there is something extraordinary about these factors in the particular case. Gender is one of the factors along with race, national origin, creed and socio-economic status, which is *never* relevant and cannot be taken into account by sentencers seeking to depart from the guideline sentence. The *Federal Sentencing Guidelines* thus attempt to eliminate gender bias from sentencing. In theory men and women who have similar records and commit similar offences should receive the same guideline sentence.

Raeder argues that the implementation of the guidelines has dramatically reduced the pre-guidelines leniency shown to women offenders and has resulted in women being sentenced more harshly than previously.[33] This outcome would have been expected if pre-guidelines sentencing discriminated in favour of women and the guidelines were intended to prevent sentencers from taking gender into account. However research by Nagel and Johnson reveals that gender is sometimes taken into account despite the guidelines.[34] An examination of three categories of offences under the guidelines shows that the possible shifts away from leniency towards female offenders have not been as marked as might have been expected. Leniency is reintroduced through the discretion still available to prosecutors in plea bargaining and to sentencers in the precise operation of the guidelines.

Drug offences

More females are sentenced for drug offences under the guidelines than for any other offence. More than one third of all women sentenced under the guidelines committed drugs offences. Women drug offenders benefit disproportionately from each of the discretionary components in the guidelines scheme which allow lower sentences.

Women are more likely to receive downward departures for 'substantial assistance given to authorities'. The guidelines authorise a downward departure where an offender has provided 'substantial assistance', for example, by providing the prosecution with information which assists them in achieving additional convictions. Women are also more likely to benefit from downward departures for 'atypical facts or circumstances', i.e. mitigating factors not adequately considered by the Sentencing Commission. Finally women are more likely to receive sentences from the low end of the applicable range.

Why do women offenders benefit disproportionately from downward departures? Nagel and Johnson suggest that the guideline sentences for some drug offences are perceived as unjust by some judges and prosecutors. Women offenders who may have a minor role[35] in an offence because of a relationship with a male ringleader are still liable under the guidelines for a substantial sentence because all participants in a conspiracy are penalised according to the total quantity of drug involved.[36] Thus judges and prosecutors attempt to find a way around the guidelines. Women offenders may not in fact provide more 'substantial assistance' than men but judges and prosecutors use this facility to secure lower penalties for women offenders whose guideline sentences appear to be 'unjust'.

The same patterns of leniency for females were observed in the offences of embezzlement and larceny with the exception that downward departures for substantial assistance were marginally more likely to be given to males rather than females. Nagel and Johnson have no explanation for this.

The results of Nagel and Johnson's research suggests that despite guidelines which specifically exclude discrimination on gender grounds, women still appear to receive more lenient sentences than men. However it is not clear that this should be explained as 'chivalry'. Nagel and Johnson do not provide an explanation for the variation in cases of embezzlement and fraud, but the explanation in drugs offences seems to be related at least partly to a perceived injustice built in to the guidelines which disproportionately affects women because of the typical position of women in the illegal drug industry. Judges exercise leniency because they perceive the guidelines as failing to take account of what they see as the reduced culpability of women in these cases.

Steffensmeier et al conducted a study of sentencing under the *Pennsylvania Guidelines* between 1985 and 1987.[37] The study collected a large sample of a wide range of common law offences controlled for seriousness of offence and criminal record. Their results show that women are marginally less likely to be imprisoned than men, but that there is no gender difference in length of imprisonment decisions. The data from interviews with sentencers asking about their reasons for downward departures from the Guideline sentence suggest that women may be considered less blameworthy and imprisonment less practicable because of child care, pregnancy, emotional problems, lesser role in the offence, remorse, and availability of jail space. Judges argued that these disparities were warranted and sensible. They reproduce both a perception of women as familial and also of women as less responsible than male offenders. The study shows equality in the length of prison sentences. This suggests that imprisonment is seen as a particularly inappropriate sentence for women (particularly conventional women in families) and that leniency may be exercised to keep women out of prison but that where imprisonment is seen as appropriate, there is little evidence of leniency being exercised. The study concludes:

> ... gender differences in court outcomes reflect a concern with maintaining the family unit and the high priority accorded to women's

> care-taking role. But the findings also suggest that gender differences in courtroom outcomes reflect real differences between male and female defendants in criminal involvement, in danger or threat to society, and in extent of health problems or mental disorder. To the extent that these gender-linked considerations are viewed as legitimate antecedents of judicial decision-making, an overall pattern of more lenient outcomes for women may still be defined as warranted and ought not necessarily to be construed as gender bias.[38]

The argument is that there must be a distinction between legitimate and illegitimate gender differences. The Guidelines prohibit any account being taken of gender *per se*. However the Guidelines do take account of the degree of involvement in an offence. It may be the case that women more frequently play a lesser part in offending than men. Thus a gender difference emerges which can in fact be explained by the degree of criminal involvement. Steffensmeier et al argue that if we take into account legitimate gender differences, there may be little remaining difference between the genders in sentencing at least where sentencing guidelines exist.[39] Of course, as Allen points out, there may be more inclination to ascribe mental disorder or health problems to women offenders.[40] The difference may not be 'real' but constructed through judicial interpretations or stereotyping. The same could apply to judicial perceptions of women as being less of a danger or threat to society.

Interestingly, a parallel study of race and sentencing by the same authors using the same data source reveals that white defendants are marginally less likely to be imprisoned than black defendants, but there is no racial difference in length of imprisonment decisions.[41] This is almost completely accounted for by dispositional departures from guidelines which favour white defendants (i.e. selecting probation rather than jail or prison). Interviews with judges provide some explanation: black offenders are more likely to be involved in drugs or to have used a weapon (i.e. factors which have not shown up in the official charges but which may influence a decision to depart or not); white defendants have better quality legal representation, and judges are reluctant to send white offenders to 'black prisons', etc. The first concerns actual behaviour rather than bias; the second concerns the allocation of legal resources to offenders, and the third is a clear example of discrimination which favours white offenders.

Frase reports studies of the effects of the *Minnesota Guidelines* on reducing race, gender and socio-economic disparities in sentencing.[42] The Guidelines were intended to provide a neutral structure for sentencing, whereby sentencers would only be able to take account of specified factors in deciding sentence, excluding gender, race and socio-economic status. Evaluations showed that disparities had been reduced. This is not surprising. Pre-Guidelines there was no structure for sentencers to adhere to. The evaluations simply measure the extent to which sentencers adhere to guidelines and, within these, how effectively they manage to prevent race, gender and socio-economic status from affecting the sentencing decision. Frase reports that although race and socio-economic disparity had been reduced, women still received less severe sanctions.[43] The research was not able to provide an explanation for this finding. In contrast, as a group minority offenders also received harsher sentences. However, this was mostly explained by their more extensive criminal histories and more serious offences.

Research into the operation of 'gender-neutral' guidelines shows that they are unable to completely eliminate gender differences in sentencing. However, the differences may not be solely due to gender but due to family responsibilities which are perceived as being disproportionately held by women offenders. It appears that sentencers, under certain circumstances, do treat women more leniently than men. Is this justifiable? The next section looks at the debate on this issue.

Equal treatment or special treatment

Should women receive equal treatment as men when being sentenced in a similar case? The debate is between those who argue that women ought to be treated equally because gender differences are irrelevant to the choice of punishment and those who argue that women should receive special treatment in sentencing to take account of the biological and cultural differences between men and women.

> The objective should not merely be to mete out equal sentences to females, but rather to guarantee that they receive just sentences which reflect their dissimilar patterns of criminality and family responsibilities.[44]

Nagel and Johnson argue that this is more properly seen as a debate about how to achieve equal treatment of women.[45] Is it to be achieved by taking into account factors which are gender-specific or by ignoring gender differences?

The *Federal Sentencing Guidelines* explicitly prohibit sentencers from taking gender into account. There has however been some case law on the issue.

Pregnancy

In the case of *US* v *Pozzy*,[46] it was held that pregnancy is not an appropriate basis for downward departure from the guideline range. In order to warrant a departure from the guidelines, physical conditions have to be extraordinary. The judgment argued that pregnancy is neither 'atypical nor unusual'.

From a desert approach, the condition of pregnancy affects neither the degree of culpability (i.e. responsibility for the criminal act), nor the harm caused by the crime. Thus the seriousness of the case (harm + culpability) is not affected. To warrant downward departures on the basis of pregnancy would privilege motherhood over the personal responsibility of female offenders.

From another perspective, it might be argued that a sentence of imprisonment imposed on a woman in the late stages of pregnancy might have negative effects on the child which would be born in prison. Pregnancy is perhaps not unusual amongst women nor amongst women offenders, however, given the vastly smaller proportion of women offenders, pregnancy is an unusual state amongst the total population of offenders. As men cannot give birth, this punishment disproportionately affects women and so women should receive special treatment to equalise the impact of punishment. This argument is based on arguments about parenthood, and particularly motherhood, which are addressed in the next section.

Parenthood

The *Sentencing Reform Act 1984* is inconsistent on the significance of 'family ties' to sentencing, reflecting the conflict which existed during the drafting of the Bill. Section 994 (d) of the Act allows the Commission to take into account family ties (among a host of other factors) if they are relevant and then only to the extent that they are relevant. This conflicts with 944 (e) which notes the 'general inappropriateness' of taking family ties into account.

The courts have interpreted the provision that family ties are not ordinarily relevant in different ways. The range of variation in the court cases referred to by Nagel and Johnson suggests that there is room for considerable judicial discretion within what are supposed to be restrictive presumptive guidelines.[47] In the case of *Goff*[48] the court did not authorise a departure for a mother of three minor children, in *Handy*[49] a departure was allowed for a single mother of an unspecified number of minor children. However Nagel and Johnson argue that the prevailing view is that single parenthood is not *in itself* an adequate basis for a downward departure i.e. single parenthood is not held to be extraordinary. This fits with a desert approach to sentencing. However, as noted earlier, there is evidence that even under the guidelines, sentencers continue to exercise leniency on women offenders particularly where those women are perceived as being responsible for the care of children. This can be justified on the basis that the social costs of incarcerating single parents in terms of the damage to the child and to the relationship outweigh any benefits of incarceration. These are utilitarian arguments which are not used by the desert approach.

An example used by Nagel and Johnson makes the point very clearly.[50] Two women clerks change pay codes to increase the salaries of employees in return for a cut and are convicted of fraud. The single woman with no children to care for receives 46 months under the guidelines, the mother who is the primary carer for two children receives 6 months home confinement under a downward departure on the basis of family ties.

From a desert perspective these cases are similar and the outcomes discriminate against non-parents including non-mothers and do not treat the two offenders equally. The approach also constructs a mother as not a fully responsible moral role and thus reinforces gender stereotypes.

From another perspective, these cases are not similar, in that the woman who is caring for children will not only suffer imprisonment, she will also have her children removed from her care and may lose custody of them for a longer period. In addition, if she is sent to prison, the children will suffer and the social costs of imprisonment could be perceived as outweighing the penal value of the custodial sentence. From this perspective punishment is seen as part of social policy. The overall gains in social policy terms are greater if the woman is not imprisoned.

Thus the definition of similarity depends on the approach taken to sentencing. In the example given, the definition given by a desert approach would condemn the sentences as unjust, the definition given by a social policy approach might welcome the sentences as promoting social justice.

The desert approach claims to be gender neutral and thus promotes equal treatment of women. The social policy approach advocates special treatment for primary care givers which in practice means special treatment for mothers. Women offenders are more likely to have primary care responsibilities for children than men whether they are single parents or not. In the USA, 88% of all single parents are women and research suggests that female inmates are more likely to have parental child care responsibilities than men. This is already recognised by sentencers who are more likely to perceive women rather than men as primary caregivers. Thus a mother may receive a non-custodial sentence to allow her to continue to look after children even though she has a live-in partner. A man is unlikely to avoid prison if he has a partner who can be held to have primary responsibility for child care. Thus, although special treatment for primary care givers does not in principle discriminate on the grounds of gender, in practice it produces special treatment for mothers.

> The gendered nature of child care responsibilities and the feminisation of poverty are grave public policy concerns that must be addressed in order to achieve a more equitable society. It is not clear, however, that the criminal sentencing system is the appropriate institution to address these pressing problems.[51]

The debate is not really about how women should be treated by the criminal justice system but about the aims and justifications of the system itself. The desert approach argues that the primary aim of a criminal justice system should be to ensure that similar offences receive similar punishment.[52] Thus the circumstances of the offender are largely irrelevant and the distribution of social welfare is seen as the concern of a separate institution. Those who see punishment as part of social policy argue that it is impossible to punish justly in an unjust society and therefore one of the main aims of the criminal justice system should be to increase social justice.[53] What counts as equality of treatment and the criteria to be taken into account in defining what counts as a similar case are bound up with particular moral and political choices about the kind of society we want to live in.

Conclusion

The principle of gender equality in sentencing fits with a desert approach to sentencing. The most coherent attempt to implement a desert approach to sentencing which is gender neutral has been in the *Federal Sentencing Act 1984*. Although research suggests that these tightly structured guidelines have reduced gender disparities in sentencing, they have not been able to eliminate them. There are areas of remaining discretion (plea bargaining between prosecution and defence, choice of sentence within the guideline range of penalties, and warranted downward departures for substantial assistance, circumstances not adequately considered by the Sentencing Commission or extraordinary circumstances) which allow traces of the pre-guideline paternalistic approach to some women offenders to persist.

Sentencers reproduce commonly held discourses about women's offending which affect their choice of sentence. Where the desert based guidelines produce a sentence which sentencers perceive as unjust for the circumstances of an individual case, they are sometimes able to get around the guidelines to produce what they see as a more appropriate sentence. This results in the persistence of some lenient treatment of women offenders. Although this is probably done to retain child care within the family rather than because women are perceived as less responsible, it has the effect of perpetuating the social construction of women as mothers rather than as rational moral agents.

It is likely to be very difficult to remove gender discrimination from sentencing practice. Sentencers appear to have a strong sense of justice which does not always coincide with a desert definition of justice. This sense of justice is partly based on particular perceptions of conventional gender roles, for example that women have primary responsibility for child care. In this case, sentencers' perceptions are confirmed by statistical data, many more women than men are primary care-givers. Whether they should be or whether the courts should recognise this fact or deal with an imaginary and for many, desirable world where men and women take equal shares in child care is a matter for continuing political debate.

One might argue that the *Sentencing Reform Act 1984* was an attempt to close this debate by drawing up a complex set of rules which was designed to impose equal treatment on women and to prevent sentencers from imposing special treatment. However, the rules required sentencers to interpret terms such as 'unusual', 'extraordinary', 'inappropriate', 'relevant'. These terms take their meaning from the context and assumptions within which they are used. A desert approach defines 'relevant' quite differently from a 'social justice' approach. Thus sentencers are sometimes able to alter the impact of apparently strict rules to produce decisions which they feel are more just. They have been able to impose special treatment on some women where the legislation was intended to implement equal treatment.

Notes

* I want to thank Denise Mina, Jane Scoular, Cyrus Tata and Malavika Vikram for their helpful comments on an earlier draft of this essay. I would also like to thank the Department of Law of the University of Dundee for inviting me to contribute to the programme of Scrymgeour Lectures in 1996.

1. von Hirsch, A., *Censure and Sanctions*, Clarendon Press, Oxford, 1993.
2. Where the principles of just desert have been applied in various forms of sentencing guidelines, the strict concentration on offence characteristics of just desert has been breached and sentencers are either permitted or required to take into account the criminal history of the offender.
3. Daly, K., 'Structure and Practice of Familial-Based Justice in a Criminal Court', *Law and Society Review*, vol. 21, 1987, pp. 267- 290.
4. Hutton, N., 'Sentencing, Rationality and Computer Technology', *Journal of Law and Society*, vol. 22, 1995, pp. 549-570.
5. Clarkson, C. and Morgan, R. (eds.), *The Politics of Sentencing Reform*, Clarendon Press, Oxford, 1995.

6. e.g. *Criminal Justice Act 1993*; Thomas, D., *Sentencing Reform: England and Wales*, 1995, in Clarkson and Morgan, *supra*, pp. 125-147.
7. Tata, C., 'Conceptions and Representations of the Sentencing Decision Process', *Journal of Law and Society*, vol. 24, 1997.
8. Hutton, N. and Tata, C., *Patterns of Custodial Sentencing in the Sheriff Court*, Scottish Office Central Research Unit, Edinburgh, 1995.
9. Hudson, B. A.,*Understanding Justice*, Open University Press, Buckingham, 1996.
10. Doob, A., 'The United States Sentencing Commission Guidelines: If you don't know where you're going, you might not get there', in Clarkson and Morgan, *supra*, 1995, pp. 199-250; also, Tonry, M., *Malign Neglect*, Oxford University Press, New York, 1995.
11. 'The 100 to 1 crack cocaine powder cocaine quantity ratio is the primary cause of the growing disparity between the sentences for black and white federal offenders': *Cocaine and Federal Sentencing Policy*, U.S. Sentensing Commission, 1995, p.21.
12. Hudson, B.A., *Understanding Justice*, Open University Press, Buckingham, 1996.
13. *Ibid.*
14. Fish, S., *There's No Such Thing As Free Speech*, Oxford University Press, Oxford, 1994.
15. Heidensohn, F., 'Gender and Crime' in Maguire, M., Morgan, R. and Reiner, R. (eds.), *The Oxford Handbook of Criminology*, Clarendon Press, Oxford, 1994, pp.997-1040.
16. There has been a sharp increase in the number of women in prison in England and Wales over the last three years: P. Cavadino, Penal Affairs Committee, letter to *the Observer*, 15 September, 1996.
17. Steffensmeier, D., Kramer, J. and Streifel, C., 'Gender and Imprisonment Decisions', *Criminology*, vol. 13, 1993, pp. 411-444.
18. *Ibid.*, p. 431.
19. Farington, D. P. and Morris, A. M., 'Sex, Sentencing and Reconviction', *British Journal of Criminology*, vol. 23, 1983, pp.229-248.
20. Simon, R. and Landis, J., *The Crimes Women Commit, the Punishments They Receive*, Lexington Books, Lexington, 1991.
21. Nagel, I. and Hagan, J., 'Gender and Crime: Offense Patterns and Criminal Court Sanctions', in Tonry, M. and Morris, N.(eds.), *Crime and Justice: An Annual Review of Research*, vol. 4, 1983, pp. 91-144.
22. Steffensmeier, Kramer and Streifel, *supra*, p. 411.
23. Allen, H., *Justice Unbalanced! Gender, Psychiatry and Judicial Decisions*, Open University Press, Milton Keynes, 1987.

24. Walklate, S., *Gender and Crime*, Prentice Hall/Harvester Wheatsheaf, London, 1995.
25. Worral, A., *Offending Women*, Routledge, London, 1990.
26. Eaton, M., *Justice for Women? Family, Court and Social Control*, Open University Press, Milton Keynes, 1986.
27. Carlen, P., *Women's Imprisonment*, Routledge and Kegan Paul, London, 1983.
28. Eaton, *supra*.
29. Walklate, *supra*, p. 140.
30. Daly, *supra*, p. 268; see also, Daly, K., *Gender, Crime and Punishment*, Yale University Press, New Haven, 1993.
31. As Daly, 1993, *ibid.*, comments, it is ironic that women's domestic labour has 'no price' and is not socially recognised as work, whereas in sentencing motherhood is socially recognised as invaluable and irreplaceable while breadwinning is not.
32. Frazier, C.E., Bock, E.W. and Henretta, J.C., 'The Role of Probation Officers in determining Gender Differences in Sentencing Severity', *Sociological Quarterly*, vol. 24, 1983, pp. 305-318.
33. Raeder, M., 'Gender and Sentencing: Single Moms, Battered Women and Other Sex-Based Anomalies in the Gender-Free World of the Federal Sentencing Guidelines', *Pepperdine Law Review*, vol. 20, 1993, pp. 905-989.
34. Nagel, I. and Johnson, B., 'The Role of Gender in a Structured Sentencing System: Equal Treatment of Policy Choices, and the Sentencing of Female Offenders under the United States Sentencing Guidelines', *Journal of Criminal Law and Criminology*, vol. 85, no.1, 1994, pp. 181-221.
35. Playing a minor role in an offence is a factor which is taken into account in the guidelines, however the guidelines only authorise a small reduction for this factor and this is insufficient (in the view of some sentencers) to bring the guideline sentences for some drug offences to a 'just' level.
36. The *Anti-Drug Abuse Act 1988* provides that all participants in a drug conspiracy are liable for the total quantity of drugs involved. The guideline sentences are anchored in the mandatory minimum sentences for particular quantities of particular drugs, e.g. 5k of cocaine = 10 years, 500gm-2000gm = 63-78 months.
37. Steffensmeier, Kramer and Streifel, *supra*.
38. *Ibid.*, p. 439.
39. *Ibid.*, p. 435.
40. Allen, H., *supra*.

41. Kramer, J. and Steffensmeir, D., 'Race and Imprisonment Decisions', *Sociological Quarterly*, vol. 34, 1993, pp. 357-376.
42. Frase, R., 'Sentencing Guidelines in Minnesota and other American States: A Progress Report', in Clarkson and Morgan, 1995, *supra*, pp. 169-198.
43. Employed offenders also received less severe sanctions. This might be explained by the sentencers'desire to maintain families by trying to limit the punishment of 'breadwinners' but Frase does not offer an explanation.
44. Raeder, *supra*, p. 909.
45. Nagel and Johnson, *supra*, p. 195.
46. *United States* v *Pozzy*, 902 F.2d 133, 138-39 (1st Cir.) cert denied, 498 U.S. 943 (1990).
47. Nagel and Johnson, *supra*.
48. *United States* v *Goff*, 907 F.2d 1441,1446 (4th Cir. 1990).
49. *United States* v *Handy*, 752 F.Supp.561 (E.D.N.Y. 1990).
50. Nagel and Johnson, *supra*, p. 206.
51. *Ibid*., p.208.
52. von Hirsch, *supra*.
53. Hudson, *supra*.

5 The Influence of European Law on Sex Equality Laws

MURIEL ROBISON, Legal Development Officer, Equal Opportunities Commission

In recent years there have been a substantial number of changes to the UK sex discrimination legislation which has resulted in significant advances toward the equality of opportunity for both women and men in Scotland. Each of these improvements to the legislation has been precipitated by the influence, both direct and indirect, of European sex equality laws.

When the UK joined the Common Market, as it was then, in 1972, membership of that community clearly involved a surrender of sovereignty in those areas which were the concern of Europe. This was a consequence of our decision to become part of the European Union. The supremacy of European Law has been confirmed both by the European Court of Justice which in 1963 in the case of *van Gend en Loos* stated that Member States had 'limited their sovereign rights',[1] and by our own courts more recently, for example, by Mr Justice Hoffmann, in the case of *Stoke-on-Trent City Council v B & Q plc*, in which he stated: 'The Treaty of Rome is the supreme law of this country, taking presidence over Acts of Parliament'.[2]

In the area of equal treatment, the Treaty of Rome, one of the founding treaties of the European Union, contains the following, Article 119:

> Each Member State shall ... maintain the application of the principle that men and women should receive equal pay for equal work.

Thus, through Article 119 of the Treaty of Rome, European law seeks to guarantee equal pay between men and women for equal work. That this principle should be enshrined in one of the founding treaties of the European Union is not a reflection of the value placed by the original Member State governments on equal pay and equal treatment, but rather the result of a concern of the French, who by 1957 already had equal pay laws, and of unfair competition from Germany, where women were paid less then men.

That was the origin of Article 119, but as the European Court of Justice has confirmed, its intention goes considerably further. Indeed, the Council of Ministers subsequently unanimously adopted a series of directives, that is secondary legislation, aimed at achieving this ultimate goal, the most relevant being the Equal Treatment Directive and the Equal Pay Directive.

In ensuring that the principle of the supremacy of European law is observed, Article 169 of the Treaty of Rome provides that the European Commission can take infringement proceedings in the European Court of Justice against a Member State in circumstances where it believes that national law has failed to implement European law, or has failed to implement it correctly. However, in recognition of the fact that the European Commission could not hope to catch every infringement, the European Court of Justice has confirmed the right of individuals to enforce the provisions of the Treaty directly. ndividuals cannot normally rely on the provisions of international treaties to give them directly enforceable rights in the courts of their own countries. The Treaty of Rome, however, as adopted in this country through the European Communities Act 1972, is an exception to that principle. The European Court of Justice has determined that where a provision of European law is sufficiently clear and precise, unconditional and unqualified, requiring no further implementing legislation, then it may be relied upon directly by individuals in the courts and tribunals of their Member State.[3] Crucially, in the field of equal treatment, the European Court has ruled that Article 119 guaranteeing equal pay could be relied upon by individuals. In the case of *Defrenne v SABENA*,[4] Miss Defrenne, an air steward on the Belgian Airline, had claimed equal pay with her male counterpart. The Court held that, as this Article created a private right, it could be enforced by individuals in their own courts and tribunals against both the state and private individuals or corporations. In European legal parlance, Article 119 has been determined to have both vertical and horizontal direct effect.

The United Kingdom relied on the previously enacted Equal Pay Act of 1970 as sufficient vehicle to allow individuals to enforce their right to equal pay. However the Equal Pay Directive, which was to be implemented by 1975, made it clear that the right to equal pay was intended to include equal pay not just for the same type of work but also for work which was of equal value.

The European Commission used its enforcement powers under Article 169 of the Treaty of Rome to take this issue before the European Court of Justice. In the case *The Commission v UK*,[5] the European Court of Justice held that the UK was in breach of its obligations under the Equal Pay Directive because the Equal Pay Act did not allow claims for equal pay for work of equal value. As a result the Equal Pay Act required to be amended, and with effect from 1 January 1984, a worker can claim not only equal pay for the same type of work but also for work which is of equal value.

The Equal Opportunities Commission has voiced its concern that the equal pay laws of this country have not achieved the objective required by European law. A brief look at the pay differentials between women and men in this country appears to provide ample evidence of that. It was for the reason of this continuing discrepancy that the Equal Opportunities Commission in 1993 took the unusual step of making a reference to the European Commission with a request that it consider further infringement proceedings using its powers under Article 169.

One important aspect of Article 119 is the very broad definition of pay:

> For the purpose of this Article, 'pay' means the ordinary basic or minimum wage or salary and any other consideration, whether in cash or in kind which the worker receives, directly or indirectly, in respect of his employment from his employer.

The European Court of Justice has confirmed that this definition of pay is very much wider and broader than our own view of pay as simply wages or salaries. One far-reaching example relates to the inclusion of occupational pensions, which are deemed to be 'pay' for the purpose of Article 119. The EOC-backed Barber case provides an interesting illustration of an individual relying directly on European law to obtain equal treatment in the benefits paid under his pension, when no remedy was available to him under national law. Mr Barber was made redundant in 1980 aged 52, after 32 years service. The normal pensionable age for employees such as Mr Barber was 62 for men and 57 for women. The severance terms provided that, in the event of redundancy, members of the pension fund who had reached the age of 55 for men and 50 for women were entitled to an immediate pension. For employees under that age the severance terms provided for a deferred pension payable at the normal retirement age. Mr Barber received a lump sum payment and a deferred pension to commence payment when he reached age 62. Had he been a woman, he would have received a lower cash lump sum, but a pension payable immediately. It was not in dispute that had he been a woman, the value of his redundancy package would have been greater. The European Court confirmed that occupational pensions were 'pay' under Article 119, and therefore that Mr Barber was entitled to equal treatment. Because neither the Equal Pay Act nor the Sex Discrimination Act cover pension benefits, those seeking to rely on the right to equal treatment in relation to pension had, until the law was changed by the recent Pensions Act of 1995, to rely solely on their rights under European law.

Thus certain aspects of the European law requiring equal treatment in pay had not been correctly implemented into domestic law. The UK government also sought to rely on the Sex Discrimination Act, which came into force on the 29th December 1975, as sufficient to implement the Equal Treatment Directive. The Equal Treatment Directive was required to be fully implemented by Member States by the 9th August 1978, that is after the Sex Discrimination Act had come into force. However, the UK government took no steps to implement the Directive, taking the view that the Sex Discrimination Act sufficiently discharged its obligations.

The Equal Treatment Directive was adopted in an attempt to secure equal treatment at work. The Directive provides that there shall be no discrimination whatsoever on the grounds of sex, either directly or indirectly, nor by reference to family or marital status, in access to employment, training, working conditions, promotion or dismissal.

Directives are secondary legislation which seek to harmonise and standardise laws throughout the European Union. They lay down minimum standards to which Member States must conform. Article 189 of the Treaty of Rome states that:

> A directive shall be binding as to the result to be achieved, upon a Member State to which it is addressed, but shall leave to the national authorities the choice of form and methods.

Thus the Member State has a wide discretion in relation to how it chooses to put the mandatory objectives of a directive into legal effect. It now transpires, however, that it was a mistake for the UK Government to rely on the provisions of the Sex Discrimination Act as sufficient to achieve the binding objectives of the Directive, that is to secure equal treatment in employment. For, in many respects, the Sex Discrimination Act has been shown to be deficient and in breach of the objective laid down by European law of achieving equality of opportunity for women and men and eliminating discrimination.

That was recognised as long ago as 1984 by the European Commission.[6] Once again using its powers under Article 169, it took infringement proceedings to air its concerns about several aspects of the Sex Discrimination Act which it considered were derogations from the principle of equality resulting from exemptions in the Sex Discrimination Act for small employers, private households, male midwives and the discriminatory provisions of collective agreements. As a result of these proceedings, the Sex Discrimination Act of 1975 was amended by the Sex Discrimination Act of 1986.

The doctrine of direct effect, which has already been mentioned in relation to Article 119 of the Treaty of Rome, allows private individuals themselves to enforce their rights under Community law in our national courts and tribunals. That doctrine also applies in certain circumstances to those seeking to rely on the legal principles laid down in directives. In what is perhaps a departure from the original intention of the Treaty, the European Court of Justice has ruled that private individuals can rely on Directives if the following conditions have been satisfied:

i. the provisions of the directives must be sufficiently clear and precise;
ii. the time limit must have passed for the Member State to implement the directive into national law;
iii. the individual must be employed by the government or an 'an emanation of the state'.[7]

As directives can be relied upon only by individuals who are employed in the public sector or in an organisation in the control of the state, but not against private individuals or corporations, they are described as having vertical, but not horizontal, direct effect.

A number of individuals in the United Kingdom have taken advantage of this principle to challenge aspects of the Sex Discrimination Act which they consider to be inconsistent with, or indeed in breach of, the European sex equality laws.

As originally enacted, the Sex Discrimination Act excluded all provisions relating to death or retirement. This meant, for example, that it was perfectly lawful for the Southampton and Southwest Hampshire Area Health Authority to dismiss Helen Marshall from her post as senior dietician at the age of 62, when male colleagues could continue working until they were 65. She found this unacceptable and approached the Equal Opportunities Commission for advice. It became clear that an argument could be mounted relying on the Equal Treatment Directive, as it appeared that Miss Marshall was employed in the public sector by an 'emanation of the state', and therefore she could rely directly on that Directive to enforce her right to equal treatment. The European Court of Justice indeed confirmed that a dismissal of a woman based on attaining the state pension age when that age was different for men is contrary to Article 5(1) of that Directive that men and women shall be guaranteed the same treatment with regard to conditions governing dismissal without discrimination on grounds of sex.[8] As a result of this decision, the Sex Discrimination Act of 1975 was further amended by the provisions of the Sex Discrimination Act of 1986, the exclusions relating to death or retirement being amended so that it is now unlawful to discriminate in the age at which men and women are compelled to retire. The Employment Protection (Consolidation) Act 1978 was also amended so that women dismissed at an earlier age than men could bring unfair dismissal claims and were entitled to redundancy payments on the same conditions as men.

Miss Marshall did not stop there however. The European Court of Justice had been asked to determine whether treatment such as that which Miss Marshall suffered amounted to discrimination. The European Court of Justice responded that it was. The procedure requires that the case is then referred back to the court which sent the original question to allow it to apply the correct law to the particular circumstances of that case. The industrial tribunal who had originally considered Miss Marshall's case found that as a result of the discrimination she had been deprived of 3 years of employment, and approximately £19,000, including interest. However, the Sex Discrimination Act specified a limit on the amount of compensation to be paid in the event of a finding of discrimination; at that time it was approximately £6,000. This was not acceptable to the tenacious Miss Marshall, who made her way, once again, to Luxembourg, where the European Court of Justice once again found that such a limit was in breach of Article 6 of the Equal Treatment Directive. The European Court of Justice ruled that, where a Member State provides a financial remedy, those who suffer discrimination must be fully compensated for their losses.

Thus Miss Marshall forced the government to change the law not once but twice. Following this decision, the government acted quickly to remove the limits on compensation and to provide for interest on awards through the Sex Discrimination and Equal Pay (Remedies) Regulations 1993, which came into effect on 22 November 1993. The limits on compensation in race discrimination cases, and on religious discrimination in Northern Ireland, were removed by subsequent legislation.

The pregnancy dismissal cases involving the Ministry of Defence have received a great deal of media attention. The Sex Discrimination Act, as originally enacted, excluded the navy, army and airforce from its remit. This meant that the MOD could lawfully discriminate against its armed forces personnel. This discrimination manifested itself in particular in its policy to dismiss automatically women personnel as soon as they became pregnant. The Equal Opportunities Commission took up the case on behalf of two former army officers, Mrs Leale and Mrs Lane, by raising an action of judicial review challenging this policy. The MOD recognised that their policy was indeed in breach of the Equal Treatment Directive and the case was settled out of court. The MOD however subsequently wrote to approximately 5,500 service women who had been dismissed, advising them to make a claim. At this time, the limit on awards of compensation was still in place, but the Marshall judgement changed things dramatically during the settlement negotiations. A combination of unique circumstances resulted in very high awards to some ex-officers who would otherwise have been highflyers in the forces.

The result was another amendment to the Sex Discrimination Act. Instead, however, of deleting section 85(4) which provided for the exemption, that section was amended from 1st February 1995 by the Sex

Discrimination Act 1975 (Application to Armed Forces etc.) Regulations 1994 as follows:

> Nothing in this Act shall render unlawful an act done for the purpose of ensuring the combat effectiveness of the naval, military or air forces of the Crown.

Concern has been expressed - both by the Equal Opportunities Commission and by leading politicians - that this does not go far enough, and that the 'combat effectiveness' defence may still be in breach of the Directive in permitting differential treatment of male and female personnel. The government issued a statement that it was relying on Article 224 of the Treaty, which allows derogation from the principle of equal treatment, amongst other things, in the event of war. The question will, in fact, be considered by an industrial tribunal in the near future. The Equal Opportunities Commission is currently supporting a case of a woman chef, made redundant from the regular army. She was offered a place as a chef in the Royal Marines which was subsequently withdrawn because the Royal Marines do not employ women in any capacity.[9] Another area where the Sex Discrimination Act was apparently deficient was in relation to discrimination which related to pregnancy in general. Tribunals in Britain originally took the view that a pregnant woman could not claim sex discrimination under the Sex Discrimination Act because the Act required comparison with a man, and such a comparison was not possible. In 1980, in *Turley v Allders Department Store*[10] the Employment Appeal Tribunal took the view that:

> When she is pregnant a woman is no longer just a woman. She is a woman with child and there is no masculine equivalent.

However, when this issue was considered again by the Employment Appeal Tribunal in 1985 it took a different view:

> The proper approach is to ask whether pregnancy (with its associated consequences) is capable of being matched by analogous circumstances (such as sickness) applying to a man.[11]

At the same time leading academics and indeed industrial tribunals in Northern Ireland[12] took the view that the correct approach was not this 'comparative approach', but rather the 'unique characteristics approach'. That approach maintained that any less favourable treatment of a woman on the grounds of her pregnancy was discrimination *per se*. As only women can get pregnant, differential treatment of them for that reason is by definition discrimination on the grounds of their sex.

In 1991, the European Court of Justice endorsed the 'unique characteristics' approach in two important cases, called *Dekker*[13] and *Hertz*.[14] In the Dekker case, Mrs Dekker had been selected as the best candidate for the job by an employment agency. When the employer found out that she was pregnant, he refused to employ her because he would not have her maternity pay reimbursed by his insurance company, as would have been the case had he known about a male's illness. The European Court of Justice said that it was discrimination not to recruit a woman by reason of her pregnancy or its consequences for the employer.

In the Hertz case, Mrs Hertz was dismissed after a considerable period of pregnancy related sick-leave, arising two years after maternity leave. The European Court of Justice held that a dismissal because of pregnancy was sex discrimination, but not where the dismissal resulted from pregnancy related illness arising a considerable time after the pregnancy when the 'comparative approach' was appropriate.

It would appear that applying the principle of supremacy of European law this 'unique characteristics' approach was the correct approach for our UK courts and tribunals to apply. However, there appeared to be a marked reluctance on the part of our courts to take such an approach. The matter came to a head with the case of *Webb v Emo Air Cargo (UK) Ltd*.[15] Mrs Webb had been taken on to be trained to replace a Mrs Stewart during her maternity leave. Two weeks after commencing the job, Mrs Webb found that she too was pregnant and would require to take maternity leave around the same time as Mrs Stewart. Mrs Webb was dismissed. When this case reached the House of Lords, the House of Lords confirmed that it is unlawful direct discrimination to dismiss a pregnant woman because she is pregnant, but it found in this case that she had not been dismissed because she was pregnant but rather because of her unavailability to attend work caused by her pregnancy. The House of Lords decided that it was appropriate to refer this issue to the European Court of

Justice and referred the question to them. In an unequivocal ruling, the European Court of Justice held that:

> There can be no question of comparing the situation of a woman who finds herself incapable, by reason of pregnancy discovered very shortly after the conclusion of the employment contract, of performing the task for which she was recruited with that of a man similarly incapable for medical or other reasons.

The European Court of Justice laid emphasis on the fact that Mrs Webb was employed on a permanent contract, and her absence through pregnancy would only prevent her on a purely temporary basis from performing the work for which she had been engaged.

The case was referred back to the House of Lords to apply the correct law as determined by the European Court of Justice. It was for the House of Lords to determine whether our Sex Discrimination Act, which apparently requires a comparison to be made with a man, could be interpreted in such a way as to accommodate the 'unique characteristics' approach required by European law in considering pregnancy discrimination. The House of Lords found that it was possible to do so.[16]

The courts in the UK have apparently been reluctant to apply European law where it is inconsistent with domestic law. Yet that reluctance to apply the principles of European law appears to be waning as evidenced, for example, in the decision by the House of Lords on the employment protection rights of part-time workers.[17] The Equal Opportunities Commission recognised the potential discriminatory effect of national laws requiring part-time workers to work for five years with the same employer before gaining protection against unfair dismissal etc., while full-time workers only required to work for two. In an action of judicial review, the House of Lords agreed that the laws discriminated against women, because most part-time workers are women, and they could not be justified. The Lords found that this differential treatment of part-time workers was in breach of Article 119, of the Equal Pay Directive and the Equal Treatment Directive.

Once again, the government was forced to change the law as a result of its incompatibility with European law. The government introduced the Employment Protection (Part-time Employees) Regulations 1995, making amendments to the Employment Protection (Consolidation) Act

1978, which came into force on 6th February 1995 ensuring that part-time workers would have the same employment protection rights as full-time workers.

A potentially far-reaching decision which also bears witness to this change is a recent decision of the Court of Appeal in the case of *R v Secretary of State for Employment ex parte Seymour-Smith and Perez*.[18] That case challenged the change in 1985 of the threshold for gaining employment protection from one year to two years, on the basis that such a requirement discriminated against women, women being less likely than men to build up two years service with the same employer for reasons of family responsibility etc. Counsel for Mrs Seymour-Smith and Mrs Perez laid heavy emphasis on the requirement of the Equal Treatment Directive that there shall be no discrimination *whatsoever* on the grounds of sex, and the Court of Appeal accepted that the two year threshold did indeed, at the time of the applicants' dismissal in 1991, discriminate against women and could not be justified. That case is to be heard by the House of Lords, and if it is upheld, it will be interesting to note whether or not the government is once again required to change the law.[19]

Our own Court of Session has perhaps not been so enlightened. It was generally agreed that the European Court of Justice had clarified the law relating to pregnancy discrimination in the case of *Webb v Emo Air Cargo*.[20] However, when it came to a decision of the Court of Session in the case of *Brown v Rentokil*,[21] the waters have been muddied once again. In that case Mrs Brown was dismissed after an absence of 16 weeks with a pregnancy related illness. As male employees in the same position would have been dismissed, there was no discrimination applying with the comparative approach. However, the European Court of Justice had by this time confirmed that there is no requirement to make comparisons with a male employee. As the reason for the dismissal was clearly related to her pregnancy, the application of that principle would indicate unlawful direct discrimination. However, the Court of Session apparently chose not to apply the line of cases from the European Court of Justice which had established the general principles, and distinguished between a dismissal relating to the pregnancy itself, and dismissal because of a pregnancy related illness which, it found, following Hertz, was not covered by the Equal Treatment Directive. Counsel for Mrs Brown had argued that the case should be referred to the European Court of Justice if their Lordships were in any doubt, but the Court of Session found that there was no requirement to do so as, in its view, the law was quite clear. That decision has been widely criticised and was recently considered by the House of Lords, which has in fact referred the case to the European Court of Justice. This will be the first referral in this area to the European Court of a Scottish Case.

In fact, there have been no references to the European Court of Justice on discrimination issues directly from courts in Scotland. This is to be contrasted with the English courts where some 40% of references to the European Court of Justice on equal treatment issues come from English courts and tribunals. It is interesting to consider why that might be. It was an issue which came up for discussion and debate at a conference which the Equal Opportunities Commission staged in June 1995 for legal professionals throughout Scotland. Judge David Edward, a Scottish advocate who is the UK representative judge on the European Court of Justice, said that there was no clear reason for this but suggested that it might be that Scottish advisers were perhaps not as sensitive to European rights as English advisers, a point echoed later in the day by another speaker, Mrs Doris Littlejohn, President of the Industrial Tribunals in Scotland. Judge Edward went on to consider why there should be more references from the UK than from any other single member state, and he suggested that this was the combined result of a general resistance to the underlying ideas of sex discrimination legislation and a slavish adherence to a literal interpretation of the statute, coupled with a failure to look at the Sex Discrimination Act in light of the Equal Treatment Directive. This may suggest the reason why cases have not been referred from the Scottish courts, as our courts have tended to take a broader and less technical approach to the interpretation of statutes than is the tradition in England.

Other aspects of the Sex Discrimination Act are still vulnerable to attack. One example where the Sex Discrimination Act's consistency with European law is to be considered by a Scottish court of Session is the case of *McMillan v The Lord Advocate*.[22] Mrs McMillan wanted to continue working part-time for her employers, the Edinburgh Voluntary Organisations Council, but she was advised that she would be required to work full-time. As she could not comply with their requirement to work full-time because of family commitments her employment was terminated. An industrial tribunal decided that she had been indirectly discriminated against, but that her employers had not intended to do so. In those circumstances, section 66(3) of the Sex Discrimination Act states that no compensation shall be payable for unintentional indirect discrimination. The tribunal held that if they had been allowed to award compensation it would have awarded her the sum of £2,250 for loss of earnings and injury to feelings. In the case of *Marshall No. 2*,[23] the European Court of Justice had confirmed that the Equal Treatment Directive required that those who suffer discrimination should be fully compensated for any losses. At the Employment Appeal Tribunal Mrs McMillan, as an employee in the voluntary sector and not in the public sector, could not rely on contradictory European laws. In other words, it was for the government to ensure that the Sex Discrimination Act was in line with the Equal Treatment Directive, and it may be that it had failed in this respect. Mrs McMillan's only option then was to sue the government in what become known as a 'Francovich' style claim[24] for the £2,250 and to argue she had lost this sum as a result of the government's failure to implement the Equal Treatment Directive correctly. In fact, this case settled following an amendment to the Sex Discrimination Act, effective from 25th March 1996, which allows tribunals to award compensation for indirect discrimination as a last resort.

As mentioned throughout this paper, the Equal Opportunities Commission has greatly contributed to the improvements in the laws relating to sex discrimination during the 20 years since it was set up. These great strides would not have been possible without the Commission's ability to challenge what we see as obstacles to the ultimate goal of equal treatment using principles of European Law.

Notes

1. *van Gend en Loos v Nederlandse Administratie der Belastingen* (case 26/62) [1963] *European Case Reports*, 1.
2. [1990] 39 *Common Market Law Reports*, 31.
3. *van Gend en Loos*, *supra*.
4. *Defrenne v SA Belge de Navigation Aerienne* (SABENA) (No.2) (case 43/75)[1965] *European Case Reports*, 455.
5. (case 165/82) [1984] *ICR*, 578.

6. *Commission of the European Communities v UK* (case 165/82) [1984] *ICR*, 192.
7. van *Duyn v The Home Office* (No.2) [1975] 3 *All England Law Reports*, 190.
8. *Marshall v Southampton and Southwest Hampshire Area Health Authority (Teaching) (No.1)* [1986] *Industrial Relations Law Reports*, 140.
9. Recent newspaper reports, for example, *The Sunday Times* of 3rd December 1995, suggest that this exemption may not be relied upon. Apparently, research scientists have concluded that there are no military roles, including those in elite forces, such as the paratroops or commandos, which women could not perform.
10. [1980] *Industrial Relations Law Reports*, 4.
11. (1) *Hayes v Malleable Working Men's Club and Institute* and (2) *Maughan v North East London Magistrates' Court Committee* [1985] *Industrial Relations Law Reports*, 367.
12. *Donnelly v Gallagher* [1978] Belfast IT Case No. 66/8650.
13. *Dekker v Stichting Vormingscentrum Voor Tonge Volwassen (VJV Centrum) plus* [1991] *Industrial Relations Law Reports*, 27.
14. *Handels - Og Kontorfunktionaerer - Nes Forbund I Danmark v Dansk Arbejosgiverforening* [1991] *Industrial Relations Law Reports*, 27.
15. [1994] *Industrial Relations Law Reports*, 482.
16. It is interesting to note that had the House of Lords found that it could not interpret the Sex Discrimination Act in line with the European judgement, then the government would have been required once again to change the law to bring it in line with European principles.
17. *R v Secretary of State for Employment ex parte Equal Opportunities Commission (and another)* [1994] *Industrial Relations Law Reports*, 176.
18. [1995] *Industrial Relations Law Reports*, 464.
19. This case was referred to the European Court of Justice on March 13th 1997.
20. *Supra*.
21. [1995] *Industrial Relations Law Reports*, 211.
22. *McMillan v The Lord Advocate* (unreported).
23. *Marshall v Southampton and Southwest Hampshire Area Health Authority (Teaching)* (no.2) [1986] *Industrial Relations Law Reports*, 140.
24. *Francovich v The Italian Republic* [1992], *Industrial Relations Law Reports*, 84.

6 Pornography and Gender Equality

PROFESSOR BEVERLEY BROWN, School of Law,
University of East London

This essay is about Catherine MacKinnon's book on pornography, *Only Words*.[1] At the heart of this book is one key idea - that pornography should be seen as a type of speech act. This essay is about why that is a brilliant idea, how that brilliant idea goes dramatically wrong, and yet why something of it is worth salvaging.

Only Words is about the power of words, and it is a powerfully written book. The very title is ironic and combative, pitched in the middle of an argument. 'Only words' is how pornography is conventionally dismissed by contrast with acts: 'Sticks and stones make break my bones, but words will never hurt me'. This is not only a homily of popular wisdom but also the nutshell version of the US First Amendment which protects freedom of speech and currently protects pornography *as* speech. It was by reference to the First Amendment that the Minneapolis Ordinance against pornography, inspired by MacKinnon and Andrea Dworkin, was struck down as unconstitutional. This book is MacKinnon's riposte.

There are two sorts of reasons why the speech-act perception is so winning. First, and despite all the gross violence that MacKinnon will inflict upon it in the course of the book, the idea of a kind of speech that does its harm solely and simply in the act of speaking itself, does capture something that falls unrepresentable in more conventional accounts of 'hate speech', including, not surprisingly, law. The fact that MacKinnon argues the case of pornography so strongly together with race 'speech' contributes to the compelling nature of her case.

Second - and this also has to do with the power of words, the 'pornography as speeech act thesis' is a brilliant argumentative manoeuvre against MacKinnon's (many) opponents, a field that includes not only conventional jurisprudence and First Amendment legal theory, but also her feminist opponents in the 'sex wars'. Where the fight with more obvious male opponents is rendered visible in a text studded with case references to back her up, the other battle is out of sight, not even conducted through footnotes, but nonetheless deeply present. For, of course, the feminism in *Only Words* is radical feminism. It is MacKinnon, after all, who pronounced the fiat 'There is no feminism but radical feminism'. Now there is a statement whose force would truly be travestied as being 'only words'.

These axes of argument and argumentation - the analytical and the acts of engagement - cannot really be separated. Where *Only Words* seeks to theorise the power of speech, it also demonstrates it. To read the book for the first time is to experience exhiliration and horror, admiration and contempt. It is, very much, to feel abused. It is to feel abused by pornography, in MacKinnon's rendition and re-enactment, but it is also to feel abused and used by the text and its author.

The task of discussing the analytics of MacKinnon's central idea is thus inextricably bound up with the question of the book's rhetoric. 'Rhetoric' is a term often applied to MacKinnon's work. Yet 'mere rhetoric' - the second sense of 'only words' - windy, unintelligible, emotional, hysterical, is precisely how, MacKinnon complains, feminist arguments are so often dismissed. Not all accounts are so uncomplimentary. Suzanne Gibson at least seeks to find an order in the MacKinnon hallmark:

> ... swoops and swirls through strings of binaries, its structure of thesis and anti-thesis, metaphor and metonymy and synecdoche: how it operates as a persuasive unanswerable rhetoric.[2]

In a rather different vein, Stanley Fish has praised MacKinnon's phrase 'ordinary rape' as exemplary of what rhetoric is about, the power of making 'a transformation in vocabulary, a change in ways of talking that effects a change in what is being talked about'.[3] Such mutations in usage, for Fish, make the difference that theories never can. Yet would MacKinnon be happy with such a characterisation of her work?

Certainly she has, in the past, very much sought to operate in the territory of high theory. Her earlier book, *Towards a Feminist Theory of the State* (1989) makes an analogy between labour in Marxist theory and sex for radical feminists ('that which is most our own, yet most taken away...'). But here too, it is the linguistic innovation - the analogy - that powers the move. And it is a powerful move, accomplishing two important goals simultaneously. By tweaking into theoretical place the familiar feminist demotics of 'sex-object' talk, she thus gains for radical feminism a certain scholarly gravitas, a weight and complexity. This is a recurring MacKinnon mode: there is always a level of address that is rooted in conventional, acceptable argumentation. Within feminism, this was also quite a political coup. For years Marxist feminists and radical feminists were at war with each other, a war expressed by completely mutually exclusive language. Suddenly, she turns it all around by finding an analogy between these two ways of talking - an analogy that will, in turn, allow Marxism - and hence Marxist feminists - to be overtaken, 'transcended' by the wider feminist perspective. Begin by agreeing with your opponent and then take the field beyond them. This is rather the lesson of martial arts: not to waste time in oppositional force, but rather to go with the opponent's momentum, to use their very strength to overpower them. A recognition of MacKinnon's ability to read and control the field of debate in turn, makes it more interesting to see what happens when it gets out of control.

Pornography and feminism

The first context of *Only Words* is the trajectory of radical feminist arguments about pornography. What has changed and what has remained the same about the position associated with MacKinnon, as well as the history of attempted social and legal reform, tells a great deal about *Only Words*.

Pornography as violence

The initial radical feminist position was centrally focused on violence, as in the famous slogan 'Pornography IS Violence to Women'. This slogan can be read in different ways. On the one hand, it can be taken as summarising a set of analytically differentiated propositions: 1) that the focal content of pornography as a genre is the depiction of violence against women; 2) that it involves sexual violence against women in its production; 3) that it causes sexual violence by influencing its male readers; 4) that pornography is a kind of discursive violence against women. The anodyne version is that this is about the circulation of images of women as objects of sexual consumption. From this point of view it would not matter whether women themselves actually saw the pornography. But there is a different version in which the point is, crucially, pornography's address to women who see it, and this will be crucial to the 'speech act' theory ultimately put forward in *Only Words*.

Taken collectively, these points are, perhaps surprisingly, convergent with conventional terms of argument, for what could fall more precisely into liberal calculations of unrestricted freedom, limited only where serious harms obtain, than the argument that pornography causes sexual violence by its users? Yet this is also tactical, for here radical feminism 'speaks' to liberalism in a language that it can understand.[4] By the same token, however, the arguments then tend to get hopelessly bogged down in disputes about causation and whether it can be established that there exists a proven link between pornography and the incidence of sexual crimes. Simultaneously, the analytical separation of the propositions goes with a disaggregating response: to deal with the problem of exploitation of performers in pornography through labour law, to treat the public visibility of pornography as a matter of indecent displays, and so on.

This propositional mode is not the only form of reading on offer here. Indeed it is quite contrary to its more radical feminist reading in which the slogan also speaks a totality that is more than the sum of the parts, in which pornography images the culture as a whole, it is as it were a hologram of the patriarchal order. Pornography is the total sign of male dominance, metonymically the part that stands for the whole, metaphorically the condensation of everything. This is precisely the sort of feminist talk that gets deemed 'unintelligible' in conventional circles as 'only words', meaningless words, ridiculous rhetoric. Yet it is a voice with considerable power.

Thus, even the early radical feminist portrayal of pornography is already an interesting rhetorical exercise considered as a multiple address to different audiences, conventional political-legal discourse and feminism. This is not to say that all feminists agreed with this portrayal. On the contrary, multiple objections were registered.[5] The emphasis on violence as the essence of male power was too crude, too obviously derived from the criminal-law thinking. The image of men as a kind of *tabula rasa* blindly acting out scenarios that pornography had imprinted on their brain was an unacceptable behaviourism. And, for those who sought to understand pornography as representation, the important issues were not the literal reenactment of acts. Radical feminism was denounced as hopelessly naive in thinking of pornography as pictures of reality, a mere representational relay that, in turn, went on to be acted out. Rather what was at stake were the regimes of visibility that structured the male gaze, the structuring of desire and the repertoire of fantasy that permeated everyday life. What was needed was an understanding of pornography as text and genre, an understanding inspired by the study of language. (And these are, precisely MacKinnon's key, unnamed opponents in *Only Words*.)

Pornography as inequality

The second moment in the development accounts of pornography ('pornography and inequality') can be seen as an answer to some of these problems. The shift in orientation to the non-criminal-law domain of civil equality and anti-sex-discrimination entailed a number of consequences. Assault was less of a paradigm and consent became more problematic. This could be characterised as a return to Weber (or, rather, the Weberianism of Kate Millett's key radical feminist text *Sexual Politics*.)[6] Instead of seeing the male order as imposed in the form of coercion, its legitimation becomes the question. Why do men (and women) accept the existing order of power and domination as worthy of obedience? Hence MacKinnon's formulation of the idea of the eroticisation of dominance.

The 'eroticisation of dominance' thesis is, simply and spectacularly, that exercising power over others, and submitting to it, has become culturally located as 'sexy'. This is, although never fully spelled out, quite a radical mutation in the classical sociological rationalism of legitimation theory, centred as it is around an act of will and a set of belief systems. While no doubt also pointing to the wider regime of beliefs supporting dominance and submission, the 'eroticisation of dominance' thesis locates the key axis of legitimation in the bodily pleasures attached to the *act* of subordination itself. Once again, MacKinnon's double address is at work, on the one hand adopting (although, of course, not mentioning) a key term from the lexicon of the social sciences, at the same time answering feminist criticisms of the crudity of the conception of masculine power as sheer physical force.

An even more obvious effect of the reign of equality law was MacKinnon's and Dworkin's almost successful attempt to create a new form of anti-pornography law, that is the Ordinances. Permitting a type of civil action, the provisions gave women, not the state, the opportunity to take the publishers of pornography to court if they had been harmed in any one of various ways by pornography. But that was a manoeuvre directly blocked by the Supreme Court.

Conventional jurisprudence

In taking on First Amendment speech doctrine, MacKinnon brings together forms of locution that seem miles apart. On the one hand, there is the full flow of radical feminist interpellation in the opening words of the text:

> Imagine that for hundreds of years your most formative traumas, your daily suffering and pain, the abuse you live through, the terror you live with, are unspeakable - not the basis of literature. You grow up with your father holding you down and covering your mouth so another man can make a horrible searing pain between your legs. When you are older, your husband ties you to the bed and drips hot wax on your nipples and brings other men to watch and makes you smile through it. Your doctor will not give you the drugs he has addicted you to unless you suck his penis. [There is a footnote here indicating that this comes from a real story.]
>
> You cannot tell anyone. When you try to speak of these things you are told it did not happen, you imagined it, you wanted it, you imagined it. Books say this. No book says what happened to you. Law says this. No law imagines what happens to you....
>
> In this thousand years of silence, the camera is invented and pictures are made of you while these things are being done ... You always know that the pictures are out there somewhere ... He has them; someone, anyone has seen you there, that way ... What he felt as he watched you as he used you is always being done again and lived again and felt again through the pictures - your violation his arousal, your torture his

> pleasure. Watching you was how he got off doing it; with the pictures he can watch you and get off any time.
>
> Slowly then suddenly it dawns on you, maybe now I will be believed.[7]

And we all know how that story will end, in legal rape, dismissal and further humiliation.

Its address is seemingly to women - but is it? Rather MacKinnon here is stamping into the realm of (male) cognition her vision of what pornography means to women. Where men express a bafflement about why pornography is taken so seriously by women, she offers a fist in the face: can you understand *this*?

On the other hand, there is the arena of First Amendment debate in which her strategy is of the variety described by Stanley Fish as 'known to every student of law':

> Despite the apparent absoluteness of the First Amendment, there are any number of ways of getting around it, ways that are known to every student of law. In general, the preferred strategy is to manipulate the distinction, essential to First Amendment jurisprudence, between speech and action.[8]

In other words, if speech is protected then, in order to remove that protection, one argues that pornography is not speech. Fish himself goes on to discuss the familiar way of doing this: the development of 'a distinction within the speech/act distinction in which some forms of speech are not really speech because their purpose is to incite violence'. In other words, here pornography is too *close* to action, too directly linked to causing physical harms, to enjoy the protection of speech. But this applies only to a very small category of utterances that take the form of injunctions *to* action. Any more general notion of ideas causing actions (that pornography causes rape) is rejected as requiring too much mediation through 'the black box of intellection'- the familiar causation problems.

MacKinnon clearly appreciates how manipulating the speech/act boundary cuts through the entire logic of the legal debate. Adopting this to place pornography, along with race-hate speech, in the category of action is a brilliant strategy, not previously dreamt of. At the same time, for the first time, it puts radical feminism into the territory of arguing about language, thus seemingly abandoning the obsession with violence and its naive 'picture theories' of pornography, linking up with equality arguments and at the same time taking over the field of feminist debate. In her hands, the brilliance of the speech act conception is that it makes the division between speech and act meaningless. On the one hand, speech acts do not express opinions. There are utterances of quite different orders. On the other hand, speech acts do not await a causal connection with the realm of action since they are already action. Pornography as a speech act thus, in conception, goes straight to the unprotected sphere of action. There is no need to go on to show a subsequent causal harm, for pornography performs its harm in its very utterance. Just like saying 'I do' in the marriage ceremony, the saying is the doing. This is evidently far more radical than the 'incitement' tactic.

To set the stage for this engagement, she first seeks to characterise the implicit theory of speech in First Amendment doctrine. Here another meaning of 'only words' appears: the surface fact of words being involved does not make them 'speech' from the First Amendment point of view. Law is not, after all, so literal minded. It is not words *per se* that are protected. Rather, it is words taken as the bearers of *ideas*, words as expressions of underlying beliefs, words as the means of conveying an opinion, words that refer to ideas. Does the text - or image - have a *content*? does it convey a *message*? Then it shall constitutionally count as speech, unless, as we have seen the message is of the order of an incitement: 'burn that house, attack those people'. MacKinnon argues that this is not the only exception.

> [S]ocial life is full of words that are legally treated as the acts they constitute without so much as a whimper from the First Amendment. ... Under bribery statutes, saying 'aye' in a legislative vote triggers a crime that can consist entirely of what people say. So does price-fixing under the anti-trust laws.[9]

Nonetheless, the 'ideas' version of pornography predominates. From the 'idea' version of pornography as speech, she traces two main consequences. First, since words are thus merely an artifact or a symbol of something else and therefore 'not real', this something else being the idea that is expressed, it means that one form of expression is as good (or as bad) as another. The particular character of pornography's *way of* speaking cannot be recognised. Second, the only instances in which a specific 'linear' chain of causation can be found between the use of pornography and sex crimes are too unique and individualised to a specific individual to be an acceptable basis of general legislative prohibition. Because ideas are general and abstract and since the same ideas about women are transmitted by other cultural forms besides pornography, law is incapable of recognising the uniqueness of pornography.

The ground thus prepared, the speech act thesis can now appear and, with it, necessarily the name of J.L. Austin in this rather remarkable footnote.

> J.L. Austin's *How to Do Things with Words* (1962) is the original enunciation of the theory of performative speech, which examines language for which 'the issuing of an utterance is the performing of an action - it is not normally thought of as just saying something,' at 6-7. While he does not confine himself to inequality, [!] which is crucial to my argument here, neither does he generalize the performative to all speech, as have many speech act theorists who came after him. Austin is less an authority for my particular development of 'doing things with words' and more a foundational exploration of the view in language theory that some speech can be action.[10]

Again, note the combination of daring and convention, for J.L. Austin is not only the inventor of the the entire theory of speech acts, but is closely linked with H.L.A. Hart in Oxford philosophy of language. Hart draws on Austin at points and, indeed, many of Austin's examples of speech acts are drawn from law. Thus MacKinnon seeks to secure her credentials, like a good lawyer herself, citing an authorised and authoritative source rather than any neo-feminist understanding. At the same time the whole note is quite extraordinary: the grudging admission that Austin may have been 'the first', the bizarre statement connecting his work to equality (this is a man who wrote about the etiquette of taking the last piece of ice cream bombe at high table), the general suggestion that he was a mere handmaiden preparing her way. Is this another of her takeover bids? Or is it perhaps, insurance against the charge that she really quite radically misunderstands, or misuses, the whole conception of a speech act?

She correctly cites Austin's definition that a speech act occurs when 'the issuing of the utterance is the performing of an action'. This is by contrast to constative utterance, statements used to assert the existence of a state of affairs which, too often, have been taken to be the key to language in general. Speech *acts rather than says* when saying the words is *itself* the performing of an action. Hence, 'I marry you', 'I promise', 'I name this ship St Catharine'. In saying those words, I am not expressing a view about what the ship is called or should be called. Rather I am actually at that moment naming it. Obviously, it is not as simple as that: there are institutional conditions about who can perform the act and in what setting. These 'felicity' conditions determine whether speaking will be a successful speech act. Sitting in my room looking at the docks and saying 'I name this ship ...' will not do.

Equally important to note, there is an important difference between an utterance itself being an act and an utterance causing acts in consequence. If my saying, 'I feel very sad today' makes you burst into tears, if my saying 'Open the door' makes you open the door, these are statements with effects but they are not speech acts, since the saying may cause the doing but the saying is not itself the doing. In Austin's terms this is the difference between perlocutionary (causal, follow-on) effects and illocutionary effects associated with speech acts proper.

How, then does MacKinnon apply this idea? First, there is an obvious connection between 'constative' utterances and speech in the Constitutional sense of being the vehicle of an idea. Yet she connects this with a different association with the word 'idea': that the consumption of pornography is in turn itself seen as intellectual, an engagement operating in the head, like being involved in a debate and, if it causes harms then, equally, these can only be harms in the head - offensiveness (which is not regarded in law as sufficient ground of restriction. Eventually this turns into an opposition between ideas and behaviour. Hence:

> ... What pornography does, it does in the real world, ...
>
> ... it is only pornography, not its ideas as such, that gives men erections that support aggression against women in particular. Put another way, an erection is neither a thought nor a feeling, but a behaviour. It is only pornography that rapists use ... This is not because they are persuaded by its ideas or even inflamed by its emotions, ... but because they are

> sexually habituated to its kick, ... primitive conditioning.... Pornography consumers are not consuming an idea any more than eating a loaf of bread is consuming the ideas on its wrapper or the ideas in its recipe.[11]

Something quite retrograde has happened. This is the same old fashioned, behaviourist vision of early radical feminism.

Even so, some sort of of speech-related thesis is argued here. It centres on the image of dogs, men as dogs:

> *Saying* 'kill' to a trained attack dog is only words. Yet it is not seen as expressing the viewpoint 'I want you dead' - which it usually does, in fact, express. It is seen as performing an act tantamount to someone's destruction, like saying 'ready, aim, fire' to a firing squad.[12]

By analogy, pornography is understood as addressed to an audience of men, most if not all of whom have been pre-socialised by a cultural diet of sexism. One is a type of causation argument that links pornography to acts rather along the lines that incitement legislation works. Here pornography is imagined as speaking to a male audience saying - as to a trained attack dog - 'Get her'. For all its radicalism, it fits the conventional rules - up to a point. First, 'Get her' could never be seen as a description or as the statement of an opinion. It is a command. Second, the trained attack dog argument deals with the argument that pornography in itself, or by itself, is not the cause of sexual violence. The cause is, rather, an audience (or even a segment of the audience) who have already been prepared, indoctrinated by the rest of the sexist culture. Third, because the statement prescribes action, there is no great leap in order to make a connection to action.

Unfortunately there are two rather less impressive things about this argument. First, it is clearly just another version of the incitement argument, already seen to be effective, but in only a very small number of situations. And, second, it is not a speech act. Commands ('Shut the door') have perlocutionary, not illocutionary effects. The entire inspiration thus degenerates.

However, there is the germ of an argument involving a speech act argument proper. This is to be found via analogies with racism, where, under the 14th Amendment (equal protection) a whole series of racist utterances have been deemed unlawful.

> Social inequality is substantially created and enforced - that is, *done* - through words and images. Social hierarchy cannot and does not exist without being embodied in meanings and expressed in communications. A sign *saying* 'White Only' is only words, but it is not legally seen as expressing the viewpoint 'we do not want Black people ...'[13]

Here, unlike the previous argument, the 'action' is not cashed out in some resultant. First of all, it is not a question of a resulting act, because the speech *is* the act. Second, and obviously, it is therefore not a question of a *physical* act. To act by speaking is not bodily conduct. But how exactly is pornography like a sign saying 'Whites Only'? Consider the question of address: to whom the words are spoken. Is the speech act in an address to men (as with the attack dog)? Well, yes, to the extent that 'Whites Only' does have an address to white people. But that is not the address that makes the analogy work. Clearly it is what the sign says to black people that is important. 'Whites Only' is not an opinion or a proposition. It is, to begin with, an implicit command, not 'Get her' but 'Get out'. But that would put it merely in the category of perlocution. What makes it a speech act proper is that it performs an act of humiliation in its very utterance. To put it slightly differently, if the sign commands 'you do not belong here', it is its further radical classification of belonging and not belonging that performs the radical distance between the I that speaks and the you who is spoken to. And so, third, to follow the analogy through, when pornography is a speech act it must be in its address to women. What it performs is an act of humiliation. It is perhaps the most unrecognised speech act of all, the act of naming. And, strangely, that is a position that MacKinnon herself might not find unacceptable - the claim that pornography performs the act of naming what sex is and shall be.

Notes

1. MacKinnon C.A., *Only Words*, Harper Collins, London, 1994.
2. Gibson, S., 'On Catharine MacKinnon', *Feminist Legal Studies*, Volume II, No. 3, 1994, p. 7.
3. Fish, S., *Doing What Comes Naturally: Change, Rhetoric and the Practice of Theory in Literary and Legal Studies*, Clarendon, Oxford, 1989, p. 48.
4. Brown, B., 'A Feminist Interest in Pornography: Some Modest Proposals' in P. Adams and E. Cowie (ed.), *The Woman in Question*, Massachusetts Institute of Technology Press, 1990 (originally published in *m/f*, 1981), Nos. 5 and 6.
5. See Smart, C., *Feminism and the Power of Law*, Routledge, London, 1989, ch 5; and Brown, B., 'Debating Pornography: The Symbolic Dimensions', *Law and Critique*, Vol. 1, No. 2, 1990.
6. Millett, K., *Sexual Politics*, Doubleday, New York, Hart-Davies, London, 1970.
7. MacKinnon C.A., *supra*, p.1.
8. Fish, S., *There's No Such Thing as Free Speech and it's a Good Thing, Too*, Oxford University Press, London, 1994, p.103.
9. MacKinnon, C.A., *supra*, p.9.
10. *Ibid.*, p. 94/86.
11. *Ibid.*, p. 11.
12. *Ibid.*, p. 9.
13. *Ibid.*, p. 9.

7 (*homo*)Sexual Citizenship

DR. DAVID T. EVANS, Senior Lecturer, Department of Sociology, University of Glasgow

In late 1993 and early '94 the impending free Commons vote on the gay male age of consent provided a concentrated example of the complex array of issues which increasingly attend all forms of sexual citizenship. The second part of this paper will be concerned with plotting the origins and parameters of what I generally mean by this term,[1] but as entrée and illustration I consider some of the key components, as revealed in this specific instance, of (*homo*)sexual citizenship.

These gay male age of consent debates encouraged pollsters to plot popular attitudes to this apparently straightforward rights issue. For example, NOP (National Opinion Polls) found 48% in favour of reduction, but of the 48% 3 times as many favoured the reduced age of 18 to 16. Thus NOP found that only 1 in 8 thought that the gay male age of consent should be lowered to the current heterosexual age, whilst 1 in 4 thought homosexuality should be banned altogether (reported *The Sunday Times* February 20th 1994).

In the media proponents and opponents of reform perceived the age of consent issue as unquestionably (whether just or unwarranted) one of 'equality'. Notable amongst the former was Sir Ian McKellen whose many media outings included the following contribution in *The Sunday Times* (January 23rd 1994): 'It is a question of human rights not numbers' he argued (referring to the '1 in 90' challenge to the long taken for granted Kinsey[2] derived claim that '1 in 10' of the population is homosexual, made by the then newly published Wellings et al survey *Sexual Behaviour in Britain* [1994]).[3] McKellen claimed that the debates which had resulted in the '67 legalisation of homosexuality under specific conditions of consent, privacy, national security, and which set the age of consent at 21, had been led by non-homosexuals wishing to protect homosexuals from blackmail. 'How the world has changed....' he observed. 'Now any number of gay men are willing to be open, so much so that (they are) vilified as "a gay lobby"-

infiltrating everywhere, and overstating the need for reform by exaggerating the numbers of gay men.' Far from challenging the new survey's '1 in 90 claim', McKellen used it and some of the survey's other findings to de-demonise male homosexuals, stating, for example, that:

> Far from being highly promiscuous, 50% of gay men have only one partner. They are unusually health conscious and practise safer-sex. They are not the disease carrying caricatures that their detractors paint ... more pertinently (he claimed), this survey shows that for many boys, homosexual activity is a normal part of growing up and establishing a sexual identity. Some will eventually define themselves as gay, most will not. ... The myth that young men can be converted to homosexuality through sexual experimentation is believed by all who oppose law reform. Yet the report suggests that it has no bearing on adult sexual orientation. (He continued): I have yet to meet the person who comes forward to say that he was 'converted' to homosexuality. Last week the British Medical Council affirmed 'sexual orientation is established early in boys and girls and appears to precede sexual activity'. Even so some gay men go to heart- breaking lengths to deny that they are innately gay ... Small wonder that when their sons 'come out', some families look for the cause or ... seducer to blame.

McKellen claimed that he knew he was gay at 12, before listing supporters of 16 'none of whom' he said 'might be tagged "gay lobbyists"' (I suppose this counts as being 'outed' as 'straight': they included Iris Murdoch, the Bishop of Edinburgh, Rabbi Julia Neuberger, Sir Terence Conran, Chris Bonington and the ubiquitous Richard Branson). He further soothed:

> ... there can be no fear of slackening the hold of heterosexuality over the national identity ... (but) the debate is about equality ... (supporters of a compromise of 18) would have the tricky job of arguing for law reform *and* discrimination. Equality they might think untenable. Would they really think they can stop youths of 16 and 17 from having sex with each other? Would they think arrest and detention desirable and practical? Would they think that such young men will care much for a society that calls them criminals for making love?

Thus McKellen employed a range of discursive elements which currently define from within the social, political, even geographical[4] immoral, space that is now gay. The pursuit of 'equality' through this single reform by a 'respectable', indeed 'normal', small and discrete (in all senses) sexual status group, membership of which is (despite apparent ambiguities) innately determined, as gay men's retrospective autobiographies including his own, 'testify', innately limits its threat to the moral community. Much hinges on refuting social constructionist arguments as 'myths' peddled by opponents of reform, myths because 'coming out' is the discovery of innate sexual self, not one possible consequence of a complex and extended negotiation of sexual preference.

Although McKellen represents the reformist wing of gay politics (*Stonewall*) his differences with more radical and disrespectful elements such as *OutRage* and *FROCS*[5] were in this instance more of reformist rhetoric and tactics than of ultimate objectives or basic beliefs for across the gay political spectrum achievement of a common age of consent at 16 was considered as unproblematically a goal of 'equality' and, as in responses to *Section 28* (*Scottish Law Statutes 1989: Local Government Act 1988*), there was a similarly uniform commitment to *essential* rather than socially constructed homosexual difference. It is no doubt a reflection of the fragmentation of gay and lesbian politics around specific issues, that great inconsistencies attend the issue of 'cause' of homosexual difference. (When confronted by such claims as Dean Hamer's 'discovery' of 'the gay gene', hostility, derision, 'so what' and relief, appeared to be voiced in equal measure, but where rights gains and losses are at stake the general tactical priority of minimising contamination risks to the 'moral host' becomes paramount, the essentialist nettle is tightly grasped and signs of the stinging pain stifled.)

Retrospectively interpreted sexual histories were also central to further media reassurances on the seduction front. *The Observer* (January 23rd 1994) reported on an Essex University survey of more than 1,000 men between the ages of 15 and 84 (presumably self-defined as homosexual although this report didn't say so), in which 88% claimed that they had first had homosexual sex before the age of 21, well over half before 16. Of those who had their first gay sexual experience between 16 and 21, 90% claimed that they had already come to recognise their sexual 'difference', not one believed that they had been, as this article stated, 'turned on' as the result of a seduction. *The Observer* concluded: 'The idea that men in their late teens are seduced into a gay lifestyle by predatory older men is a fantasy. ... The majority of men have their first sexual experience with boys or men of the same age. The average difference in age is just one year. The average age of first gay sex is 15 years 7 months, the average age of first anal intercourse 20 years 9 months.' Such mainstream media accounts present a seemingly authoritative challenging sense of what is 'normal' and of the weaknesses of laws banning consensual sexual behaviours.

Edwina Currie and Janet Daley addressed the gay social, moral and political space from the outside, representing respectively liberal sponsorship and conservative opposition. Like McKellen, Currie (*The Times* January 13th 1994) also emphasised the pragmatic case for 16 in the wake of the Conservative Party's 'back to basics' confusion of the preceding 2-3 months which led *The Times* to ask the following day: 'Is it part of the State's task to regulate sexual behaviour?' (January 14th 1994). Currie emphasised the distinction between criminal and immoral behaviours: 'No doubt many colleagues along with the public deplore the whole idea of homosexuality. That doesn't mean we should ban it'. Currie made it clear why causalist considerations must override the moralist with laws governing consensual sexual behaviours, observing that:

> ... current law inhibits the underaged from complaining about unwanted gay advances, it forces silence and not protection for it is the young themselves who would be questioned and possibly implicated ... the Department of Health (cannot) warn of HIV dangers to those underaged and thus breaking the law ... (and the) 18 compromise would be 'unjust', for the simple reason that a 17 year old male is considered able to give his consent to a sexual relationship with a female but not with a male?

Thus Currie's pragmatic recommendation for legal change accompanied affirmation of homosexuality's moral stigma, but asserted that legal 'justice' and morality need not, do not and should not, coincide. She continued:

> Here is an outmoded law which touches, at the most conservative estimate, a million of our fellow citizens who are gay. They pay their taxes and hold down jobs; their ranks have included distinguished actors, composers, writers and artists, politicians and soldiers. They run banks and businesses at the highest level. Yet on this one topic their personal judgement is regarded as dangerous; the state decides who they may and may not love.

So again de-demonisation was attempted. There is the substitution of *love* for *sex*, and the immorality of the homosexual contextualised as a personal judgement by people otherwise esteemed, and given some kind of material identity. Indeed she was more democratic, for she added; 'The welfare and human rights of a large group of our voters are at stake', before referring to trends towards equalisation in other 'civilised' societies, and amongst the many media accounts echoing this sentiment several made telling comparisons with Eire's recent dramatic conversion. August 17th 1993 saw legalisation of male homosexuality and at the common age of consent of 17, nor were exceptions made for the armed services or merchant navy as they had been in *The Sexual Offences Act* (England and Wales) of 1967. Sexual orientation was incorporated into the *Unfair Dismissals Act* and with in addition, incorporation of sexual orientation into the 1990 *Prohibition of Incitement to Hatred Act*, Eire lays fair claim to being formally the most liberal of all European societies in this area of legislation, but as Alexandra Duval Smith in *The Guardian* ('Shamrock Pink' February 8th 1994) emphasised, outside Dublin (where the pink punt is much in evidence 'in the pockets of lesbians and gay men in the arts, business, and media worlds and in night clubs where unusually cohesive lesbian and gay communities dance together') the situation is very different. In Dublin too outside of such discrete commercial territories, 'there is violence in and around gay cruising areas, and discrimination'.

This reference to the pink punt reminds us that the economic dimension is central to differential citizenship status and rights and thus to the contemporary material construction of homosexuality: the gay economy, the gay market, the pink dollar, pound, franc, punt etc.. For example *The Sunday Times* (23rd November 1994: 'Deeply in the Pink') reported how in the USA advertising now enthusiastically appeals to 'gay dinkies' (double income no kids) and 'the less attractively named sinkies' (single income no kids). Research carried out in 1993 by Overlooked Opinions of Chicago claimed that gay men in America had an average household income of $53,325 p.a. compared to a national average of $36,520, leading major companies to fight for advertising space in America's gay press and targeting gay readers in the 'straight press' (for example, the furniture company IKEA). Here on February 2nd 1996 between the two halves of ITN's *News at Ten* a three minute Peugeot advert for its new 406 model flirted with the all male kiss, showing two men kissing, a first for a British

TV ad. *The Times* reported that it 'was designed to be confused with a kiss of life', quoting a Peugeot spokesman: 'We are saying, you can be whatever you want to be' (*The Times* February 17 1996). In March *Virgin Vodka* was promoted on certain Sky channels with a male kiss from which 'kiss of life' confusion is apparently absent.

Consumer boycotts have also shown 'pink' market power. In 1990 the gay pressure group *Act-Up* implemented a ban on Marlboro cigarettes and Miller beer at US gay venues because the parent company Philip Morris had donated $200,000 to Senator Jesse Helms 'family values' campaign' (*The Sunday Times* August 22nd 1993). In Britain gay magazines such as *Attitude* and *Gay Times* have become glossily commodified carrying ads for many mainstream products such as Benetton, Absolut and Smirnoff Vodkas, Fiat and Toyota cars etc. Each November Olympia or Earls Court in London hosts the *Gay Lifestyle* exhibition, that of '93 being billed as '3 floors of fun and entertainment', which crystallises the distinct parameters of what passes for the 'gay community' (in London at least), boasting stands selling sports clubs, travel, hotels, bars, health education, charities, business and financial services, legal advice, clothes, sex toys etc. The fashion conscious leisure and lifestyle consumption character of this 'community' is seen by many as an ideal testing ground for mainstream companies new products. Ivan Massow, labelled as 'gay financial adviser', claimed somewhat ominously in *The Sunday Times*, as subsequent traumatised male letter writers were to testify (August 22nd 1993):

> What gay men wear today, straight men will wear tomorrow. Companies would do well to test their products on the gay market. I suppose you could argue that gay men are being exploited, but its a two way thing. There is a definite advantage in being recognised, even if it is *only* as consumers.

This article also described how central, coded, idealised images of the body are to this commercialisation:

> Over the past couple of years, Calvin Klein has used shrewdly provocative ads for jeans and underwear, where the clothing is almost an intrusion on the image of the naked male, Levi's, Jordache and others (have run) similarly chic, if less steamy campaigns. Banana Republic has a series of ads in which boys and boys and girls and girls caress in

androgynous affection. These campaigns run in mainstream media like *Vanity Fair* and if middle America has not got the message it certainly has every opportunity to do so.

A Hollywood producer explaining the box office success of *Philadelphia*, was quoted: 'It doesn't matter who you sleep with or what you sleep with ... they care if you make money.' But it does matter, if you are 'out', where you live, work, drink, eat, holiday, where you spend your money and with whom, and where, as Duval Smith's article on Eire reminded us, you encroach on general, 'normal' 'moral' public space, be it 'cruising' Phoenix Park in Dublin, working in Hollywood film studios or serving as members of the British armed forces etc.

Market forces may amorally test moral and legal boundaries in the interest of expanding commodification and exploitation, but the consequence is not the incorporation of the immoral into moral society, but instead the development of discretely managed and policed markets which materially underpin the legal/immoral social space occupied by minority sexual status groups.

Gay populations are in their social, leisure and lifestyles, part- time, corralled into what have become largely self-regulating distinct territories which at their outer limits are policed not only by the police themselves and those who prey on this vulnerable population when thus exposed, but more comprehensively by the persistent reiteration of the immorality of those within, their lower esteem and honour as citizens, whatever their legal status. Indeed the gradual extension of rights facilitates this segregation, gay social and commercial sites increasingly drawing into them, under the banners of 'liberation' and 'equality' rhetoric, the morally stigmatised, re-affirming their innate difference from those in the 'moral' heterosexual and immorality condemning community outside.

It is deeply ironic that in these debates about sexual rights, sexual radicals defensively adopt a conventional stance on the origins of sexual orientation, whilst their conservative opponents, as McKellen rightly conceded, become aggressively radical social constructionists. Janet Daley (*The Times* January 27th 1994) affirmed her opposition to age of consent reform on the grounds that: 'the immaturity of adolescent boys makes them more suggestible and manipulatable than girls and this is an excellent reason for not making them the legal objects of seduction - even by their peers'. She also objected to:

> ... the politicisation of homosexual life (for it) greatly increases the dangers in which adolescents may be put (it) locks people into what might have been a transitory stage in their development, a commitment which ... cuts them off from parenthood. To be gay is now seen as being part of a movement. Having once signed up it is disloyal to deny your membership ... Instead of encouraging freedom and flexibility, gay activism implies that, once homosexual or bisexual you should forever count yourself part of the 'gay community'...

... the existence of which she scorns:

> 'what they have in common is more the result of their lack of family responsibilities than their sex lives. For the insecure and the uninformed, such certainty of self image (based on occasional and experimental sex acts) can be fatally attractive'.

Finally she claimed that the hostile response of some gay activists to the Wellings *et al*[6] '1 in 90' claim suggests that:

> ... what (they) want is to present homosexuality as an alternative 'normality' and not an insignificant minority ... and yet it is quite unlike mainstream heterosexual normality in its insistence that what you do in bed is what you are: that your sex life is not an incidental fact about you, but your essence.

So Daley's social constructionist views focused on gay *sex* not *love*, by definition outside family values and extended beyond sexual 'seduction' to what might be called a political and lifestyle seduction thesis: gay political discourses plus cultural segregation and distinctiveness encouraging a rigidity in self definition and policing rationalised by 'commitment of self' to essential sexual difference.

Other opponents of reform also welcomed the '1 in 90' finding as proof beyond all doubt that 'the gay lobby' has an influence in and on the 'moral community' out of all proportion to the size of the population it purports to represent, a lobby further vilified for winning an unjust proportion of the health budget to combat and treat AIDS and for misleading the public on AIDS data, making false or exaggerated claims about the threat of HIV contamination to heterosexuals, and simultaneously underplaying its own 'lifestyle' induced pollution. Opponents sugared their invective of course with generous declarations of friendship to the, in these new statistical circumstances, surprisingly many of the '1 in 90' they claimed had already crossed their paths: Daley for example, stated 'there have always been gay men amongst my most treasured friends'.

Out of these extracts from media debates attending the Commons vote on the gay male age of consent the contemporary parameters of (*homo*)sexual citizenship may be summarised as follows:

(i) ... the existence of a sexual status-group, its members primarily identified by homosexual orientation and/or activity ...

(ii) ... the origins of its sexual difference ascribed, defensively and conservatively, to innate factors by those within and supporters without,[7] but, albeit inconsistently, to social influences by conservative opposition without ...

(iii) A sexual status group increasingly defined by a particular constellation of civil, political and social rights, but which incorporate its continuing immorality and ...

(iv) ... which normally consigns the group's 'open' or 'out' presence to distinct formally and informally defined and policed territories or spaces set apart from the 'moral community',...

(v) ... territories concerned with a range of 'community' social, sexual and political services but increasingly dominated by the consumption of gay leisure and lifestyle commodities, 'fun and entertainment' as the *Gay Lifestyle* exhibitions sell it,...

(vi) ... territories which play host to *other* less developed but developing 'immoral' sexual status groups: lesbians, male and female bisexuals, transvestites, transsexuals etc....

(vii) ... territories which are home to 'liberation' and 'equality' rhetoric in overtly political and 'common-sense' everyday discourses.

(viii) For most group members, participation in these territories is 'part- (i.e. leisure/consumption) time', the territories themselves usually dispersed and diverse, idiosyncratic structural characteristics which make the term 'the gay community', used generally and unthinkingly in the media as descriptively accurate and by gay politicians of all political colours as another form of defensive rhetoric, at least problematic.

(ix) From these territories specifically political parties and arguments develop, but the 'politicisation' Daley deplores: the firming up of a distinct sub-culture and 'commitment of self' to homosexual identity and group membership is effected not only by explicitly political, but also these routine commercial leisure and life-style discourses and practices,...

(x) ... leaving explicitly political campaigns over such issues as the one in question here, relatively rare, and, when they do occur, likely to attract minority active support even when mobilised through the mythic rhetoric of 'equality'.

I have used terms such as 'predominantly', 'primarily', and 'normally', because I do not wish to argue *either* that all homosexual populations, *or* the citizenship processes with which they are variously engaged, are as neatly confined as this summary example suggests, indeed the dynamics of sexual citizenship occur in arenas of considerable personal as well as group diversity, arenas of at least potential conflict and resistance, but I am keen to convey that advancement into homosexual identity and subculture is generally and 'normally' an advancement into material citizenship constraints, distinct moral norms and responsibilities as well as rights, limited participation in segregated, privatised social and economic territories, advancement beyond which is, for the majority, either of no great concern, and/or entails moral costs which are simply too high to pay. I have also repeatedly used the term 'increasingly', which clearly conveys my view of future developments.

In brief: (*homo*)sexual citizenship consists of the dynamic development of a particular constellation of rights and responsibilities which grant a specific sexual population permission to enter, as Massow has recognised, a sub-culture of exploited consumers, the great majority of whom willingly buy their lesser sexual status.

In order to address the origins and parameters of sexual citizenship in general, as they apply to other sexual minorities as well as to male homosexuals, I shall now concentrate on five elements present in the debates already referred to:

Firstly, the widespread acceptance of innate sexual difference by the populations concerned, a key element in their defence against charges of contamination of the 'moral' population and as such in their material construction, their social, moral and economic confinement.

Secondly, the distinction drawn between, and practical separation of, legality from morality which creates and defines the 'immoral' social space occupied by sexual minority groups, within which they are confined.

Thirdly, the forms of civil, political and social rights which define and confirm this space and which...

Fourthly, determine access to and constraints on the specific leisure and life-style markets which thereby develop, leading to...

Fifthly, political incorporation or depoliticisation so that the contradictions between institutionalised, segregated, limited citizenship experience resting on affirmed innate difference, and 'equality' rhetoric become unrecognised and unobserved.

So back to the first of these. As we have heard, a fundamental contested theme of gay male age of consent debates has been the *origin* of sexual difference, nature versus nurture, innateness versus social construction, the possibility of sexual *re*orientation through seduction or experimentation, negotiation even choice, with, ironically, proponents of legal change adopting the former conventional position as conservative opposition dramatises 'contamination' threats through recourse to the radical latter. The irony is many layered, not least because sociology, which with other related disciplines has, with growing evidence and conviction during the past 20 years, espoused the constructionist case as 'challenging' and 'subversive', (arguing in the process that the social construction of sexualities is critically facilitated by the 'blind' commitment of populations affected to essentialist explanations), finds itself sharing a bed, albeit uncomfortably, with the guardians of the moral community, as, in McKellen's terms, 'peddlers of myth'.

When talking to sociologists and other social scientists specialising in the study of sexualities, I am frequently berated for unnecessarily repeating, even basically, the development of the constructionist paradigm, for surely, I am told, we are 'all social constructionists now'. Experience confirms, however, that for the great majority the constructionist case is not only not well known, it remains personally, politically and intellectually almost as challenging as it was when first broached 20 to 30 years ago. Indeed, amongst the converted there is by no means agreement on the parameters of what therefore remains for many no more than a paradigmatic article of faith.[8] For the purposes of this lecture, therefore, it is necessary to reiterate some basic detail here, which also serves to indicate my departure point *en route* to the destination of sexual citizenship.

Sociology's *credo* vis-à-vis sexuality emerged most suggestively in the pioneering essay 'The homosexual role' by Mary MacIntosh of 1968 which analysed the sociological implications of the Kinsey data[9] of some twenty years earlier, demonstrating that the significant variations charted by Kinsey in the same populations' sexual behaviours over both short and long periods of time, were dependent on the influence of situational location and differential exposure to cultural influences. 'An identifiable constructionist approach dates from this period',[10] most systematically in the work of symbolic interactionists (Gagnon and Simon in the USA and Plummer in Britain) who somewhat self-consciously asserted their terms of engagement as challenging. For example, Gagnon and Simon claimed in '73[11] that 'the sexual may be precisely that realm wherein the superordinate position of the socio-cultural order over the biological level is most complete', that 'sexuality is subject to socio-cultural moulding to a degree surpassed by few other forms of human behaviour' whilst for Plummer: 'nothing is sexual but naming it makes it so. Sexuality is a social construction learnt with others'[12] but, given the weight of essentialist opinion, as Carol S. Vance recounted in 1989: 'the struggle to move away from essentialist and naturalizing ways of thinking about sexuality has been a difficult one'.[13] Symbolic interactionism concentrated on middle range and especially micro-aspects of socio-sexual construction and learning, emphasising the dynamic emergence (via constant individual negotiations with significant others in various contexts), of identities characterised by behaviours, acts, allegiances, motives, interests, rationalisations, etc. The theatrical metaphor was central: actors interpreting scripts, giving performances, improvising to degrees, on stages with other actors. Thus 'the individual learns to be sexual as he or she learns sexual scripts, scripts that invest actors and situations with erotic content'.[14] A hyperactive learning process which initially interactionism weakly sought to stabilise through the calming effects of, for example, repetition, routinisation, 'commitment of self'. In part this hyperactivity was due to the fact that so preoccupied were Gagnon, Simon and Plummer with the elaborate social scripting and fluidity of sexuality: labelling, 'coming out' processes, movement from primary to secondary deviance in 'immoral careers' and situationally induced renegotiations of acts, identities and meanings (as in for example, single sex institutions such as prisons, schools, the military, certain work environments etc.), they rarely raised their sights to encompass the macro-material theatre in which all the performances were/are taking place. Plummer made muted references to an 'objective reality' which he did not define, Gagnon and Simon eventually by 1986 to 'cultural scenarios', their 'objective reality' equivalent, details of which they also left to others to pursue.[15] By the 1990s, as I will briefly discuss later, this interactionist concern for stabilisation of sexual negotiations within a formally rendered 'objective reality', has become stifled, crushed even, with the embrace by some leading exponents of postmodernism.[16] Despite all such problems, however, interactionist research has convinced, as had McIntosh's analyses of Kinsey data, together with burgeoning cross-cultural, anthropological and transhistorical studies, that sexualities are not innately fixed or universally patterned.

If interactionism demonstrated the social construction of sexualities at the individual and small group level Michel Foucault's dramatic intervention through his discursive approach to sexuality as introduced in the first volume of his planned *History of Sexuality: The Will to Know*[17] sought to explain at the macro-level the escalating sexualisation of modern societies, the explosion of sexual scripts or discourses, within which the diffuse, micro 'intricate local understandings of the workings of power'[18] are located. Foucault proclaimed: 'sexuality has become the medium through which people seek to define their personalities and ... to be conscious of themselves'.[19] In the modern era, the 'truth' about sexuality is delivered by 'experts' and 'saviours' in forms of instructional discourse or knowledge. Bodies' dimensions are measured, symptoms and treatments isolated; 'types' catalogued; acts accounted and trained for; dysfunctions treated, as we seek our 'innermost', 'unique', essential sexual souls, cleansed through the verbalisation of desires, practices, guilt, shame, embarrassment, innocence, inexperience and so on, in various professional 'expert' but especially media, inter-personal and subjective secular confessionals.

As a result sexuality becomes associated with everything requiring explanation no matter how minor or apparently nonsexual, indeed sexuality in a conventional sense tends to evaporate, for sexual discourses serve as instruments of domination in the modern regime of 'bio-power', which 'groups together in an artificial unity ... anatomical elements, biological functions, conducts, sensations, and pleasures, and (makes) use of this fictitious unity as a causal principle, an omnipresent meaning, a secret to be discovered everywhere'.[20]

As the power references indicate *The Will to Know* was also 'a *re*elaboration of a theory of power',[21] away from the formal and juridical, and towards immanent normative forms. It is thus a history of subjection both with regard to the creation of the subject and the internalisation of normative control into the deepest recesses of subjectivity: the sexual. In the modern era the 'natural subject' and sexuality beyond the constraints of language and culture have not been formally repressed by legal prohibition, denial and censorship as dominant wisdom would have us believe (Freud 1977,[22] Reich,[23] Marcuse[24] and Marcus[25]), but have rather been discursively elaborated. Sexually we are what we learn, internalise and reproduce as knowledge and the language through which knowledge is understood. We are subjects of the power immanently installed in that knowledge. Foucault claims to track the latest (possibly final) stage in the imperialism of a rationalising society seeking to attribute a status and definition to everything even the unclassifiable: the epitome of the 'personal', 'private', and 'mysterious', that which most naturally resists the cultural: sexuality, the most important source of identity for modern subjects, and therefore the ultimate means of their/our complete subjection.

In one sense Foucault's text is little more than an unnecessarily obscure unsubstantiated polemic statement of the obvious. The sexualisation of modern societies is accepted on all sides of all debates and more succinctly described elsewhere as, for example, being hooked on *The Sexual Fix*[26] or as 'worshipping at the altar of sex religion' (Greer 1984)[27] since 'the rutting revolution'[28] of the 'permissive 60s' but this would be to belie Foucault's persuasive concentration on the driven subjectivity of this sexualisation process and its considerable polemical influence (for example, it has been claimed that it 'dramatically changed the field of sexual history'[29] and its effect on sociology and other disciplines has been no less great). More damagingly to dispose of Foucault so readily is to avoid responding specifically to his shortcomings, particularly those pertinent to the analysis of forms of sexual citizenship, such as the following four:

(a) Firstly, if interactionist logic results in a hyperactive sexual actor in a power vacuum, Foucault's logic leads to an actor so suffused with power-knowledge that he/she does not *act* in any social or conscious sense at all. Sociology remains in the words of Max Weber: 'a science which attempts the interpretative understanding of social action in order thereby to arrive at a causal explanation of its cause and effects'.[30] Social action is 'all human behaviour to which the acting individual attaches subjective meanings, action being social when by virtue of the subjective meanings attached to it by the acting individual (or individuals) it takes account of the behaviour of others and is thereby oriented in its course'.[31] Thus, the basic unit of analysis is the orientation of the individual actor either singly or in aggregate which, in providing a meaning of anticipated reciprocal significance of action, bestows upon that action a social quality. Weber employed the term 'social relationship' to denote: 'the behaviour of a plurality of actors insofar as, in its meaningful content, the action of each takes account of that of others and is oriented in these terms...'. Therefore, as a defining criterion, it is essential that there should be at least a 'minimum of mutual orientation of the action of each to that of the others. The content may be of the most varied nature: conflict, hostility, sexual attraction, friendship, loyalty or economic exchange.[32]

For Marx too, human activities though constrained, limited, determined by aggregate forces and material conditions which lie beyond their individual wills, are still conscious activities: 'Man makes his life activity itself an object of his will and consciousness. He has a conscious life activity (which) distinguishes man from the life activity of animals. Only for this reason is his activity free activity'.[33] Foucault's preoccupation with 'the (immanent) completeness of power in its micrological aspects' eradicates human agency and leaves us with knowledge pre-programmed sexual automatons who, and this is the second shortcoming....

(b) ... as such cannot question or resist. Despite the objections of self-styled hagiographers such as Halperin.[34] Foucault's rejection of the repressive thesis with its reliance on the imposition of formal laws and institutions, inevitably leads him to also reject 'liberation' goals, indeed they appear central to the deception, to seek or gain 'liberation' is to become further embroiled in the discursive web. As one critic has observed: 'All objects and human beings exist within relations of power, even those who resist, who set their faces against what appears to be the norm, participate in the production of the norm in the very act of opposing it, by allowing the norm to be articulated against its abnormal opposite'.[35] Foucault's references to 'reverse' and 'counter' discourses may suggest resistance but he leaves little room for any, as he himself acknowledged with some regret in his last writings and interviews.[36] In *The Will to Know* he states 'the irony of this deployment of sexuality is in having us believe that our "liberation" is in the balance'.[37] Rights language and 'liberation' sentiments merely mystify the processes of social domination, falsely constructing autonomous self-determining subjects. Our visions of freedom, and our pursuit of perpetual spirals of pleasure 'are complicit with the powers we would oppose'.[38] Counter discourses are little more than demonstrations by subjects that they have been colonised by sufficient power/ knowledge to be left to police themselves. To make this criticism of Foucault is not to reject the significance of immanent normative power in the construction of sexualities, nor the incorporating tendencies within many if not most 'reverse' discourses, but to remind us not only that as social actors we are engaged, as interactionism describes, in *negotiation*s and *emergence*, but also that, as interactionism fails to acknowledge, we do so within social structures marked by formal machineries of political and economic, (that is material) power which subject us to contradictory and inconsistent discourses of which we must actively make sense. This brings us to the third and fourth criticisms:

(c) Thirdly, Foucault's critique of the repressive thesis was particularly concerned to pour scorn on Marxist and Freudian-Marxist naive reductions of sexual repression to capitalism's changing labour requirements, but his unwillingness to do more than credit the Bourgeoisie with almost inadvertently discovering this bio-political concern for self-preservation, inheritance of wealth etc.[39] is irritating and inadequate though his polemical intent is clear: no matter how much we may apparently differ in our tangible and formal assets, we are all but bit players in the grand march of discursive history. We do not have to think very long or hard, however, to recognise numerous ways in which differential economic power influences actors' participation in all aspects of this regime of 'bio-power'. A regime now surely heavily dependent upon the marketing, sale and purchase of 'its secret' - from the consumption of designer orphans and in vitro fertilised babies, to hard-core computer pornography, transsexual surgery, paedophile tourism, the purchase of expensive leather and bondage wear etc.

(d) Fourthly, Foucault's rejection of formal power models and the role of the modern state is equally inadequate. If we merely consider the four major discursive channels within the capitalist epoch (somewhat arbitrarily identified by him) leading to the construction of the sexually innocent child, the Malthusian couple, the gynaecological woman, and the sexual deviant, they are manifestly channels through which the state has expanded its formal citizenship monitoring powers, as a tariff of current disputes within the first of these four demonstrates: sex education in schools, corporal punishment, children's rights to divorce parents, the 'underaged' male child's ability to knowingly rape or sexually assault, child sex abuse within the family, the workings of the child support agency, pre-school nursery provision, and the gay male age of consent. You may also recall recent cabinet minister talk of sexual streaming in schools to minimise the contamination of the sexually innocent by the precocious alongside advocacy of free condom provision to all female school children of 12 and older.

By avoiding the formal mechanisms of market and state in the material construction of sexualities, Foucault presents a singular discursive onslaught against which his actor is helpless. In practice, however, political and economic discourses are neither mutually consistent nor reinforcing, they are tense, fragmented, contradictory, at times in outright conflict as the amoral tendencies of the market confront the moral dilemmas, inconsistencies or resilience of a state which for the past 30 years has policed sexualities according to causalist rather than moralist principles, largely divorced legal justice from morality and thereby opened up a social, moral, legal space in which actors negotiate with the 'contradictory and inconsistent discourses' to which they are subjected.

Let us now turn to the second of the five elements which aids our understanding of the development of sexual citizenship: the separation of legality from morality.

The late '50s and notorious '60s were the catalyst years in the emergent political, economic and moral battles for discursive dominance over sexual citizens and sexual consumerism, a period of unprecedented legal reform, affluence, burgeoning leisure and lifestyle consumption, which asserted sexuality as an 'autonomous sphere of pleasure and self expression with its own intrinsic value and justification ... in the context of mutual consent and respect'.[40] The most outstanding document of this 'era of the legislation of consent'[41] was *The Wolfenden Report*[42] which drew the distinction between 'private morality' and 'public good', between crime and sin, as follows: '... it is not the function of the law to interfere in the private lives of citizens, or to seek to enhance any particular pattern of behaviour',[43] yet it is still the law's duty to 'preserve public order and ...':

> ... decency, to protect the citizen from what is offensive and injurious, and to provide safeguards against the exploitation and corruption of others ... Unless a deliberate attempt is made by society, acting through the agency of the law, to equate the sphere of crime with that of sin, there must remain a realm of private morality and immorality which is not the law's business.[44]

The recommended change in legal emphasis was from moral to causal judgements: 'if it turns out that more harm is done by forbidding an activity than by allowing it, then Parliament will permit it, even if most of the members consider that activity to be wrong or immoral'.[45] Male homosexuals and female prostitutes were the test-cases specified. The intention was not to weaken moral values: Wolfenden described homosexuality as 'reprehensible from the point of view of harm to the family'[46] and emphasised that public manifestations should be severely policed. However a legal/immoral space was created in terms of degrees of legal and/or moral deviance, civil, political and social rights, economic power etc.. In the words of Mort[47] 'Discourses hierarchise and distribute the various categories of sexual deviance around the norm of marriage, the family and procreation, which provide the 'particular regime of truth' around which have developed 'incommensurate and irreconcilable conceptions of the (sexual) good',[48] and accordingly facilitated incommensurate and irreconcilable conceptions of consumable identities, lifestyles and 'communities' with enforcement at the boundaries.

Whilst this legal retreat from immorality on grounds of 'consent' and 'privacy' has become the norm, there is by no means consensus that this should be so, nor the complete absence of legislation which readdresses the link between sin and crime. For example, in response to *The Times* question referred to earlier (January 14th 1994) 'Is it part of the state's task to regulate sexual behaviour', Professor John Finnis claimed: 'A political community that judges that the stability and educative generosity of family life is of fundamental importance, can rightly judge that it has a compelling interest in doing whatever it can to discourage (homosexual) conduct'. But Finnis not only ignored the baleful, amoral commercial pressure on sexual legal and moral boundaries to enhance the size of exploitable populations and the profitability of 'immoral' commodities, he passed over 'this political community's', or rather moral state's increasingly interventionist acknowledgement that 'the stability and educative generosity of family life' can no longer be 'naturally' left under parental or patriarchal control, and that here too as the protection of children draws them into the citizenship fray, commercial forces place additional pressures on their rights as proto-citizens, as proto-consumers.

We have also had *Section 28* and *Operation Spanner*, both of interest in this context, the former a strange hybrid piece of legislation, which, as far as I know, has yet to be formally enacted, its strength seemingly not legal but moral, an inhibiting reiteration of the necessary cultural confinement of the most developed form of family threatening sexuality. By contrast *Operation Spanner* appeared initially to mark a reversal of post-Wolfenden policy, but this successful prosecution of consenting 'victimless' participants in acts of sado-masochism, now appears to have been only a temporary reversal: 2 of the 5 appeal Law Lords did not support the original conviction, last December (1995) the European Commission of Human Rights ruled that an appeal against conviction by the accused was admissible under the European Convention on Human Rights, whilst, also last December the Law Commission addressed sado-masochism by consenting adults in its second detailed consultation paper on the issue of consent in the Criminal Law.[49] With *Operation Spanner* citizenship status clearly depends on judgements of criminality *and* immorality, but a successful appeal would release S/M populations into the legal/immoral space currently occupied by other forms of minority sexual citizenship.

This brings us to the third of the five elements: the meaning of citizenship.

In a minimal classical sense 'citizens ... are all who share in the civic life of ruling and of being ruled' [50] having the right to be consulted on the conduct of the political society 'and the duty of having something to contribute to the general consultation'[51] being 'bound by the results ... for duties flow from ... rights'.[52] Thus, idealised citizenship is a matter of simple inclusionary principles of a respectful contractual relationship between autonomous moral subjects and their state. In practice, however, citizenship has developed as elaborate tariffs of partial or complete exclusion according to standards of status and moral conformity. Such shopping lists of rights as the European Convention on Human Rights (1948)[53] apart from providing a political and moral contextualisation of citizenship battles, do not equate with the differential experiences of citizens for reasons which the liberal accounts of Rawls[54] and T.H. Marshall implicitly identify.[55]

It is with some trepidation that I refer to the former here, but Rawls[56] identifies four socially valued stages in the emergent properties of citizenship rights in their constitutional and institutional forms.[57] The first consists of those primary goods (social and natural) which any rational person would want 'whatever his plan of life or social orientation would be'.[58]

Social primary goods form the basis of all citizenship and include 'the basic liberties':[59] freedom of thought and liberty of the conscience, indispensable to the protection of determinate conceptions of the good within the limits of justice, freedom of movement and free choice of occupation against a background of diverse opportunities; powers and prerogatives of offices and positions of responsibility which 'give scope to various self-governing and social capacities of the self';[60] income and wealth (defined broadly as 'all purposive means'[61] having an exchange value), and finally, the social bases of self respect - in general those aspects of basic institutions normally essential 'if citizens are to have a lively sense of their own worth as persons and to be able to develop and exercise their moral power and to advance their aims and ends with self- confidence'.[62] Natural primary goods include health and vigour, intelligence and imagination, qualities dependent upon primary social goods.[63]

Rawls locates these primary goods in their specific social contexts as he moves through his other three stages, the second consisting of two 'principles of justice', the first of which is phrased as a right: (i) Liberties arranged so as to achieve the most extensive justifiable set of equal basic liberties for each and everyone. (ii) Social and economic inequalities arranged so that (a) they are structured by social roles and offices, which are open to all under conditions of 'fair equality of opportunity' and such inequalities in wealth, income and position serve (b) to improve, ideally to maximise, the life situation of the least advantaged group.[64]

Rawls third stage is the identification of how (and the extent to which) these two principles of justice are brought to bear on the distribution of primary goods, through any particular society's economic, political and other institutions so that rights and duties are assigned and monitored.

The fourth stage concerns 'the legitimate expectations' of populations; the extent to which a particular citizenship culture is accepted as given and in which injustices in constitutional rights, or state practices are challenged.

To these four stages Rawls adds what he calls the general 'method of effective equilibrium' meaning that in any particular society rights machineries will be mediated by accumulated historical and cultural assessments of what is being done, how it is being done and why it is being done.

By extracting key terms, this summary clearly defines the machineries and experiences of citizenship as restrictive on particular subjects 'self-confidence' and 'sense of self-worth', 'plan of life', 'scope for self-government', realisation and expression of 'social capacities of the self' etc. on the grounds of particular disqualifying, in this instance, sexual, 'orientations'. Similarly, linking these '*egalitarian*' principles of justice to market constraints of wealth and income, as together part of overall '*legitimate expectations*', affirms the interrelationship between the two spheres. Also a causal relativism is implicit, for once such citizenship principles are established, the history of citizenship rights, whatever the peculiarities of any one society's method of '*reflective equilibrium*', will consist of battles over the legitimacy of *relative* claims. The post-Wolfenden reforms released handicapped (because immoral) sexual status groups into a relativist-causalist citizenship fray.

T.H. Marshall's analysis of citizenship within the capitalist era as an evolutionary democratisation of *civil*, through *political* to *social* rights also explains the grounds for legitimate partial disqualification, but does so more simply by describing social rights as: 'the right to share to the full in the social heritage and to live the life of a civilised being *according to the standards prevailing in the society*'.[65] T.H. Marshall recognised that this civilised life included market access and choice by referring to the work of late 19th century commentator Alfred Marshall who, for example, advocated

> of consent for homosexuals should be reduced to the same age as that for heterosexuals.[79]

There was also much emphasis on the need to resist 'self-oppression' due to the internalisation of psychoanalytic models of normality, on what was called 'gender bending' as well as sexual experimentation, all of which overtly carried a social constructionist agenda: rejection of sexual discourses which proclaimed the constraints of nature. Sexuality was a dynamic social construct to be negotiated with through the making of personal/political choices, not an essence with which one had to come to terms. In the post-*GLF* '70s and '80's this constructionist impetus in gay politics became submerged as first 'respectable' parties (such as *CHE* and *SMG* later *SHRG*[80] and then *OutRight*) employed more conventional political means to achieve 'reformist' political ends, concentrating on the provision of social as well as support territories and services, but these too gradually lost their impetus and their membership as commercial interests, some but not all gay owned, moved in to exploit a market with, as we now realise, enormous potential. By 1977 Weeks observed: 'the days of the euphoric (gay) rally to arms are over ... the most creative work of Gay Liberation in the ... future will come from a multiplicity of relatively small groups burrowing through their specialised concerns than from a massive new national initiative'.[81] But *GLF* had never attracted 'a massive' following, and in general the number formally 'active' in gay political parties of all colours has continued to decline. True there has been 'burrowing' of the type predicted by Weeks in a few, and for the tabloid press, notorious 'loony' local authorities[82] as well as over a range of citizenship issues: age of consent, rights of marriage, adoption, child custody, tax status, job discrimination, law enforcement and police practices in punitive control and non provision of protection, censorship, an array of rights issues related to AIDS, for a period opposition to *Section 28*, plus the occasional 'spectacular' (threatened) 'outing' of high clergy and MPs. But the majority presence has been on the gay commercial scene, the 'massive new national initiative' *Lifestyle* exhibitions at Olympia. Gay 'pride' is for most a commercial pride, 'liberation': the freedom to choose which of a narrow range of gay commodities to consume, the modern gay subject, first and foremost, a consumer in specialised markets shared by others whose qualifying presence and participation is believed to rest on their essential sexual difference.

To those such as Simon,[83] Weeks[84] and Plummer[85] for whom late modernism, or postmodernism, has fragmented and deconstructed all sexualities including the homosexual, leaving material economic, political and legal structures and constraints as relatively unimportant in determining the organisation and experience of human sexualities, my analysis will no doubt appear old-fashioned and thus largely irrelevant. Indeed there are very few contemporary sociological texts on sexuality in which due deference is paid to Marx and Weber. Neither may have specifically addressed sexuality, but both in grand style describe the world in which populations' sexualities are learnt and lived. I must admit that I am no believer in postmodernism as a distinct historical epoch or condition, but it certainly exists as contemporary chic, hip, undisciplined, interdisciplinary paradigm. For example, I find it rich, to now see such interactionists as Simon,[86] after years of frantically trying to respond to criticisms of lack of material context and disregard for the 'objective reality' in which sexual interactions take place, suggesting their analyses were, from the beginning, percipient of the postmodern sexual condition. In practice the scope for any sexual actor to resist or ignore the material contexts in which (s)he lives is extremely limited, if possible at all. Market relations impose collective routinised order on sexual life-styles behind the façade of the fetishised individualism of the consumer. Political policies, legal statutes and practices impose collective routinised moral and spatial order on sexual life chances behind the façade of the fetishised sovereign citizen. In the context of (*homo*)sexual citizenship the result is a worldwide network of 'gay villages' and a culture of breathtaking narrowness, consensus and uniformity.

Under such blatant manifestations of the material formalities of sexual citizenship it is also misleading to argue that 'alternative and contested dimensions to sexual citizenship' (in old style interactionist language *negotiations* by individuals and groups) and 'sexual stories of intimate citizenship'[87] 'harbour the potential for political change'.[88] To such as Weeks and Plummer my analysis will thus also weigh heavily as unduly 'nihilist',[89] but, I am afraid, this is where the research evidence leads. Legal/immoral sexual populations undoubtedly negotiate with and within the material constraints placed upon them, and in doing so develop 'intimate' interactional rationalisations and commitments which reflect on what it is that binds them together, but their negotiations lead for the great majority to consensus and conformity to the formal material constraints of sexual citizenship, constraints made all the more effective by the belief that what binds (homo)sexual 'communities' together is their essential sexual difference. These are thus negotiations in which the potential for political change is severely and materially constrained.

This strengthened commitment in gay politics to anti-social constructionist essentialism no doubt has no single, simple, straightforward explanation, but the material development of sexual citizenship as I have described it here is fundamentally complicit. Citizenship machineries are constructed around notions of the naturalness of conventional socio-sexual morality, the unnaturalness of difference. Sexual citizenship 'advance' is dependent on minimalisation of potential contaminations to the moral host, including assertions of essential difference, the ability to responsibly and discretely police self. In our culture many mandarin and most 'common-sense' discourses on sexualities continue to be driven by a biological mandate; 'sexuality', 'love', 'romance', 'attraction', 'satisfaction', 'guilt', the entire regime of 'bio-power', are elaborated, especially in commodified terms, through mystifying references to the fetishised individual searching for her or his own personally unique sexual secret. In such a context constructionist arguments are quite simply too individually and collectively subversive, they challenge the 'world taken for granted' paradigm which reveres absolute moral standards and citizenship justice. Amanda Udis-Kessler[90] has argued that before the Stonewall riots, to achieve acceptance, gay politics attempted to show heterosexual society how similar heterosexuals and homosexuals were, or at least could be if freed from the oppressive constraints of nature. The idea of sub- or countercultural difference was not common in the decades before Stonewall, after which lesbians and gay men, encouraged by the development of segregated territories in which to express and consume their distinct lifestyles, moved from assimilationism to what she calls an 'ethnic' model of oppression and counterculture, perceiving themselves as akin to a racial minority in a white racist society. They drew on civil rights language, developing equivalent 'ethnic' explanations of oppression such as 'homophobia' to strengthen the parallel with racism.[91] As this 'ethnic' minority, lesbians and gay men began to stress the difference between themselves and heterosexuals, and to root this difference in biology.[92] Social constructionism, with its fluidity and connotations of choice threatened lesbians and gay men as soon as it was proposed for (by arguing that sexuality could not be compared to skin colour as a natural phenomenon) it questioned their greatest asset, the ethnic self-conception, the certainty that they knew who and what they were, failed to offer a sound replacement and made them vulnerable to political opponents thus able to argue that lesbians and gay men could change and perhaps should be forced to do so, and that they had the capacity unless controlled to convert or subvert others, especially the more vulnerable. 'While constructionist theories have been preaching the gospel that the hetero/homo sexual distinction is a social fiction, gays and lesbians in everyday life and in political action, have been hardening the categories'[93] and in so doing have confined themselves to not only distinct fetishised 'ethnic subcultures' and identities, but to material forms of sexual citizenship which formalise and re-affirm their immorality, their lower esteem and contain the threat they pose to the moral community, and its 'particular regime of truth'.

Notes

1. Evans, D. T., *Sexual Citizenship: The Material Construction of Sexualities*, Routledge, London and New York, 1993.
2. Kinsey, A. C., Pomeroy, W. B. and Martin, C. E., *Sexual Behaviour in the Human Male*, Philadelphia, 1948; W.B. Saunders, *Sexual Behaviour in the Human Female*, Philadelphia, 1953.
3. Wellings, K. et al, *Sexual Behaviour in Britain: The National Survey of Sexual Attitudes & Lifestyle*, Penguin, London, 1994.
4. See for example, Bell, D. and Valentine, G., *Mapping Desire: geographies of sexualities*, Routledge, London, 1995.
5. FROCS= Faggots Rooting Out Closeted Sexualities.
6. Wellings, K. et al, *Sexual Behaviour in Britain: The National Survey of Sexual Attitudes & Lifestyles*, Penguin, London, 1994.
7. Various writers argue that from the late nineteenth century onwards gay and lesbian subjects embraced the essentialist paradigm as an overtly political defence. See Halperin, D. M., *Saint Foucault: Towards a Gay Hagiography*, Oxford, New York, 1995.
8. See Stein, E., *Forms of Desire: Sexual Orientation and the Social Constructionist Controversy*, Routledge, London, 1992.
9. McIntosh, M., 'The Homosexual Role', *Social Problems*, 16, 2, 1968, pp. 182-192; Kinsey, A. C., 1948; Saunders, W.B., 1953.
10. Vance, C. S., 'Social construction theory: problems in the history of sexuality',in D. Altman *et al., Which Homosexuality? Essays from the*

International Scientific Conference on Lesbian and Gay Studies, Gay, London and Amsterdam, 1989, p. 20.

11. Gagnon, J.H. and Simon, W.S., *Sexual Conduct: The Social Sources of Human Sexuality*, Aldine, Chicago, 1973.
12. Plummer, K., *Sexual Stigma*, RKP, London, 1975.
13. Vance, C. S., *supra*, p. 20.
14. Gagnon, J.H. and Simon, W. S., 'Psychosexual development', *Transaction*, March 1969, pp. 9-17.
15. Gagnon, J.H. and Simon, W. S. 'Sexual Scripts: permanence and change', *Archives of Sexual Behaviour*, April 1986, pp. 97-121.
16. Simon, W. S., *Postmodern Sexualities*, Routledge, New York and London, 1996.
17. Foucault, M., *The History of Sexuality: Volume One: An Introduction*, Penguin, Allan Lane, Harmondsworth, 1981. 'The Will to Know' is a translation of the original title 'La Volonté de Savoir'.
18. Marshall, B., *Coming on Strong: Gay Politics and Culture*, Hyman/Unwin, London, 1989, p. 268.
19. Foucault, M. and Sennett, R., 'Sexuality and solitude', *Humanities in Review*, 1981, pp. 3-21.
20. Foucault, M., *The History of Sexuality: Volume One An Introduction*, Penguin, Harmondsworth Allen Lane, 1981, p. 154.
21. *Ibid.*, p.187.
22. Freud, S., 'Three Essays on Sexuality' in A. Richards (ed), *Sigmund Freud: Volume 7: On Sexuality*, Penguin, Harmondsworth, 1977.
23. Reich, W., *The Function of the Orgasm*, New York, 1961; Farrar, Strauss and Giroux; Reich, W., *The Sexual Revolution: Towards a Self-governing Character Structure*, New York, 1969.
24. Marcuse, H., *One-dimensional Man*, Beacon Press, Boston, 1964; Marcuse, H., *Essay on Liberation*, Beacon Press, Boston, 1969; Marcuse, H., *Eros and Civilisation, a philosophical enquiry into Freud*, Beacon Press, Boston, 1974.
25. Marcus, S., *The Other Victorians: A Study of Sexuality and Pornography in Mid-nineteenth-century England*, Weidenfeld and Nicolson, London, 1966.
26. Heath, S., *The Sexual Fix*, Macmillan, London, 1982.
27. Greer, G., *Sex and Destiny: The Politics of Human Fertility*, Secker and Warburg, London, 1984.
28. Amis, M., 'Making sense of AIDS', *The Observer*, 23 June 1985, p. 22.
29. Gilbert, A., 'Review of M. Foucault The History of Sexuality, Volume One: An Introduction', *American Historical Review*, 84, 1979, pp. 1020-1.

30. Weber, M., *The Theory of Economic and Political Organisations*, Free Press, Glencoe Ill, 1947, p. 110.
31. *Ibid.*, p. 110.
32. *Ibid.*, p. 118.
33. Quoted in Frankl, G., *The Failure of the Sexual Revolution*, Kahn and Averill, Hove, 1974, p. 22.
34. Halperin, D. M., *supra*.
35. Haug, F., *Female Sexualisation*, Verso, London, 1987, p. 196.
36. See e.g. Kritzman, L.D. (ed.), *Michel Foucault: Politics, Philosophy, Culture. Interviews and Other Writings, 1977-84*, Routledge, London, 1988.
37. See note 17.
38. Comay, R., 'Excavating the repressive hypothesis: aporias of liberation in Foucault', *Telos* 67, 1986, pp. 111-119.
39. 'Death was gradually ceasing to torment life so directly. ... Western man was gradually learning what it meant to be a living species in a living world, to have a body, conditions of existence, probabilities of life. ...' [1981, pp.142-143] see note 17.
40. Seidman, S., 'Transfiguring sexual identity; AIDS and the contemporary construction of sexuality', *Theory, Culture and Society*, 6, 1989, pp. 293-315, at p. 298.
41. Hall, S., 'Reformism and the legislation of consent', in National Deviancy Conference (ed.), *Permissiveness and Control*, Macmillan, London, 1979.
42. (*Wolfenden Report*) *The Report of the Committee on Homosexual Offences and Prostitution*, Cmnd 247, HMSO, London, 1957.
43. *Ibid.*, p. 10.
44. *Ibid.*, pp. 9-10, 24.
45. Davies, C., *Permissive Britain: Social Change in the Sixties and Seventies*, Pitman, London, 1975, p. 3.
46. *Wolfenden Report*, *supra*, para. 124.
47. Mort, F., *Dangerous Sexualities: Medico-moral Politics in England Since 1830*, Routledge & Kegan Paul, London, 1987.
48. *Wolfenden Report*, *supra*, para. 124.
49. The Law Commission, *Consent in the Criminal Law: A Consultation Paper*, Law Commission Consultation Paper No 139, HMSO, Norwich, 1995.
50. Aristotle, *Politics*, Penguin, Harmonsworth, 1972, p. 45.
51. Brogan, D.W., *Citizenship Today*, University of Carolina Press, Chapel Hill, 1960, p. 4.
52. Brogan, D.W., *supra*, p.5.

53. For a full discussion see Robertson, A.H. and Merrills, J.G., *Human Rights in Europe: A Study of the European Convention on Human Rights*, Manchester University Press, Manchester, 1993.
54. Rawls, J., *A Theory of Justice*, Oxford University Press, Oxford, 1972, and 'The Basic Liberties and Their Priorities' in McMurrin, S. (ed.), *Liberty Equality and Law*, Cambridge University Press, Salt Lake City and Cambridge, 1987.
55. Marshall, T. H., *Citizenship and Social Class and Other Essays*, Cambridge University Press, Cambridge, 1950, p. 38.
56. Rawls, J., *supra*, at p.21.
57. *Ibid.*, p. 21.
58. *Ibid.*, p. 31.
59. *Ibid.*, p. 22.
60. *Ibid.*, p. 23.
61. *Ibid.*, pp. 22-23.
62. *Ibid.*, p. 22.
63. *Ibid.*, pp. 62, 303.
64. *Ibid.*, pp.60,83,250, 302-303.
65. Marshall, T. H., *Citizenship and Social Class and Other Essays*, Cambridge University Press, Cambridge, 1950, p.28.
66. *Ibid.*, p. 6.
67. *Ibid.*, p. 6.
68. See Mort, F., 1987, p. 45.
69. Rawls, J., 'The basic liberties and their priority' in S. McMurrin (ed.), *Liberty, Equality and the Law*, University of Utah Press/Cambridge University Press, Salt Lake City and Cambridge, 1987, p. 18.
70. Weber, M., 'Class, status and party' in Gerth, H.H. and Miller, C.W. (eds.), *From Max Weber*, RKP, London, 1967, p. 181.
71. Bauman, Z., 'Sociology and postmodernity', *Sociological Review*, 36, 1988, pp. 790-813.
72. Foucault, M. and Sennett, R. (1981), 'Sexuality and solitude', *Humanities in Review*, 1, pp. 3- 21 at p. 18.
73. Heath, S., *The Sexual Fix*, London, Macmillan, 1982.
74. Featherstone, M., 'Body and consumer culture', *Theory, Culture and Society*, 1983, p. 2.
75. p. 29.
76. Hobsbawm, E., 'The formal march of labour halted?: or observations on the debate' in M. Jacques and F. Mulhern (eds), *Observations on the Debate*, New Left Books, London, 1981, p. 2.

77. Tucker, S., 'Sex, Death and Free Speech', *Body Politic*, 58, November 1979, p. 12.
78. Watney, S., 'The ideology of the GLF' in Gay Left Collective (ed.), *Homosexuality, Power and Politics*, Allison and Busby, London, 1980, p. 64.
79. (*GLF London Manifesto* 1970.)
80. CHE = Campaign for Homosexual Equality. SMG = Scottish Minorities Group. SHRG = Scottish Homosexual Rights Group.
81. Weeks, J., *Coming Out. Homosexual Politics in Britain From the Nineteenth Century to the Present*, Quartet, London, 1977, p.234.
82. Cooper, D., *Sexing the City: Lesbian & Gay politics within the Activist State*, Rivers Oram Press, London, 1994.
83. Simon, W. S., *Postmodern Sexualities*, Routledge, New York and London, 1996.
84. Weeks, J., *Invented Moralities: Sexual Values in an Age of Uncertainty*, Polity, Cambridge, 1995.
85. Plummer, K., *Modern Homosexualities: fragments of lesbian and gay experience*, Routledge, London, 1992 and Plummer, K., *Telling Sexual Stories: Power, Change and Social Worlds*, Routledge, London and New York, 1995.
86. Simon, W. S., *Postmodern Sexualities*, Routledge, New York and London, 1996.
87. Plummer, K., *supra*, p. 151.
88. At p. 147.
89. *Ibid.*
90. Udis-Kessler, A., 'The borderline bisexual blues', in J. Geller (ed.), *Bisexuality: A Reader and Sourcebook*, Times Change Press, New York, 1990.
91. Weinberg, G., *Society and the Healthy Homosexual*, Anchor Books, New York, 1973.
92. Horowitz, A., 'Beyond the gay nation: Where are we marching?', *Out/Look*, 1, Spring 1988, pp. 7- 21.
93. Epstein, S., 'Gay politics, ethnic identity. The limits of social constructionism', *Socialist Review*, 93/4, May, 1987, p.12.